JUDY

Creative Marbling on Fabric

A Guide to Making One-of-a-Kind Fabrics

Martingale
& COMPANY

BOTHELL, WASHINGTON

FIBER
STUDIO
PRESS

Martingale
& COMPANY

CREDITS

President . . . . Nancy J. Martin
CEO/Publisher . . . . Daniel J. Martin
Associate Publisher . . . . Jane Hamada
Editorial Director . . . . Mary V. Green
Technical Editor . . . . Melissa Atkins Lowe
Design and Production Manager . . . . Cheryl Stevenson
Cover and Text Designer . . . . Trina Stahl
Copy Editor . . . . Liz McGehee
Illustrator . . . . Laurel Strand
Photographer . . . . Brent Kane

Fiber Studio Press is an imprint of Martingale & Company.

MISSION STATEMENT

We are dedicated to providing quality products and service by working together to inspire creativity and to enrich the lives we touch.

Creative Marbling on Fabric: A Guide to Making One-of-a-Kind Fabrics
© 1999 by Judy Simmons
Martingale & Company, PO Box 118, Bothell, WA 98041-0118 USA

Printed in Canada
04 03 02 01 00 99   6 5 4 3 2

Library of Congress Cataloging-in-Publication Data
Simmons, Judy
Creative marbling on fabric : a guide to making one-of-a-kind fabrics / Judy Simmons.
p.   cm.
Includes bibliographical references and index.
ISBN 1-56477-256-X
1. Textile painting.   2. Marbling.   I. Title.
TT851 .S585 1999
746.6—dc21   98-49819
                                                                              CIP

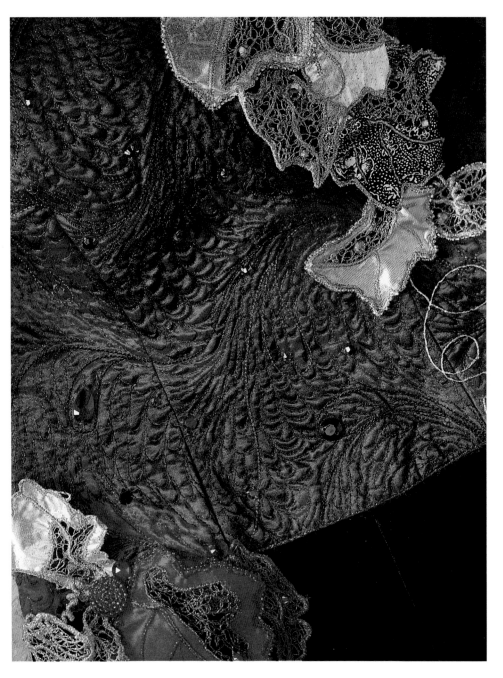

ACKNOWLEDGMENTS

♦ To my family, for your patience, emotional support, and just pitching in to do the "mom" stuff so I could stick with this.

♦ To my husband, John, for building so many marbling trays and understanding my enthusiasm for wanting them right that moment.

♦ To Dan and Cornelia Carpenter, for your friendship, support, and incredible computer expertise.

♦ To my students, who have received this art form with such enthusiasm and have made teaching such a pleasure.

♦ To the staff at Martingale & Company—your enthusiasm and talents are inspiring. It's been a joy working with each and every one of you.

♦ To my editor, Melissa Lowe, for making my words sound wonderful and for keeping me grounded through the "ups and downs."

♦ To Brent Kane, for your incredible talent and ability to make every photograph a work of art.

♦ To Bernina of America, for all your support and for creating a sewing machine that is a joy to use.

♦ To Mimi Schleicher, for being my inspiration, mentor, and friend over the years. Mimi, your incredible talent is only surpassed by your warm and sharing personality.

♦ To Barbara Butler, for her wonderful class, "No Templates Required," which inspired the project on page 80.

Contents

Introduction

IAM ALWAYS FASCINATED by personal stories, especially those that describe how the artist began his or her journey into art. Sometimes the artist spends a lifetime pursuing one area of art, and sometimes the artist simply happens into something that immediately captivates them. In my case, it was the latter.

For years, my husband and I have attended the annual Southern Highlands Craft Guild Art Show in Asheville, North Carolina. Several years ago, I happened to see artist Mimi Schleicher demonstrate the process of marbling paper. Like most people, I'd seen marbled paper used as end papers in leather books, but I didn't know anything about the process. I was amazed and mesmerized by Mimi's demonstration. Although she worked primarily with paper, Mimi had marbled fabric, and she enthusiastically shared what she'd learned.

Thus the adventure began. My husband made marbling trays; I made rakes and combs. I ordered the basic supplies and was off and running. My first efforts at marbling were all too wonderful, or so I thought! I realize now that my enthusiasm far exceeded my abilities.

I learned to marble the hard way—through trial and error. The advantage to trial and error is you learn what not to do, as well as what to do, and it's unlikely you'll make the same mistake twice. My goal in writing this book is to help you understand the process of marbling; hopefully, to help you learn from my mistakes; and finally, to inspire you to experiment. No matter what your experience or skill level, you can create beautiful, unique marbled fabric.

I love the creative aspect of marbling as well as the technical process. Marbling is in and of itself exquisite, but when mixed with other areas of surface design, it takes on a new dimension. I love combining marbling with other surface-design techniques, such as painting, dyeing, printing, stamping, and applying resists. This book has instructions and ideas to guide you through the basics of marbling, and through using many other surface-design techniques with marbling.

The marbling process can be simple or complex. The projects featured in this book cover both ends of the spectrum: luxurious fabric created with limited time and space, and challenging techniques using large trays and rakes. Whatever direction your journey takes, I hope the adventure will be fun and rewarding. May you love each piece of fabric you create (or at least get a good laugh) and enjoy using each piece in your creative pursuits.

Judy Simmons

A Brief History

Marbling is a printing process. Pigments are placed on a tray filled with a thickened solution, then raked into designs using a stylus, rake, or comb. The fabric is lowered onto the raked pigments to make the print. The final step is to heat-set the pigments on the dry fabric.

MANY HISTORIANS HAVE traced the story of this beautiful art form, but when and where marbling first started is unclear. Albert Haemmerle, considered to be the greatest authority on early decorative papers, believes that an early form of marbling may have been practiced in China during or prior to the Ming dynasty (1368 to 1644).

Today, many of us are familiar with a related method, Japanese suminagashi. *Sumi* means "ink" and *nagashi* means "float." In suminagashi, the artist applies inks to unthickened water in a tank or bath, then creates patterns by fanning or blowing (through straws) on the inks. Unfortunately, the inks begin to spread and sink as soon as they make contact with water, so the artist has little control.

Ebru, an art commonly practiced in fifteenth-century Turkey and Persia, is more similar to the marbling we will do in this book. Like marbling itself, the origin of the word *ebru,* or "cloud painting," is unclear. Some historians believe that the word derives from the Persian word *ebr,* "cloud," while others believe it derives from the term *ab-ru,* "water surface." In ebru, the artist used a mucilaginous material to thicken the water. The thicker water base, combined with thicker oil and gouache paints, gave the artist much greater control over the pattern.

First used to decorate handmade paper and embellish manuscripts, marbling became important as a method to prevent forgery in the Ottoman Empire. The pattern could not be erased without obvious results; therefore any documents written on such a paper could not be changed. Thus, the actual marbling methods and patterns were closely guarded secrets.

During the sixteenth and seventeenth centuries, interest in this art form slowly spread throughout Europe. By the seventeenth century, artists in Germany, France, Holland, and England had begun using and creating marbled papers. Some of the patterns shown in this book date to this period.

By the eighteenth century, marbling had made its way to the Americas, where it became fairly common in books and pamphlets. Benjamin Franklin insisted that part of the twenty-dollar bill be marbled to prevent forgery.

Marbling methods and patterns remained mostly secret, however, as craftsmen sought to prevent competition. Many masters taught an apprentice only one step of the craft and isolated their apprentices from each other so the steps could be kept secret. In fact, some master craftsmen called themselves magicians and claimed that they used secret formulas to create marbled papers.

In 1853, Englishman Charles Woolnough, a self-taught marbler, published *The Art of Marbling.* At last, the process of marbling was revealed. Woolnough describes marbling as "an art which consists in the production of certain patterns and effects, by means of colors so prepared as to float upon a preparation of mucilaginous liquid, possessing certain antagonistic properties to the colors prepared for the purpose, and which colors when so prepared, floated, and formed into patterns upon the surface of the liquid, are taken off by laying thereon a piece or sheet of paper, or dipping therein the smoothly cut edges of a book."

Woolnough's book remained the leading text on the craft until 1885, when Joseph Halfer of Budapest refined the process and published *Die Fortschritte der Marmorierkunst,* later published in English as *The Progress of Marbling Art.* While Halfer's work renewed interest and enthusiasm in marbling, the craft gradually gave way to mechanized forms of book production and dwindled to an obscure book art.

Today, marbling is enjoying a revival in fiber arts as more artists become aware of this magical craft. The materials used to make the marbling base, or size (water mixed with thickeners so the paints will float on top), and the paints are a bit different, but the methods and patterns are much the same. As you work, I hope you'll spend just a moment thinking of marbling's incredible history—and your possible contribution to its future.

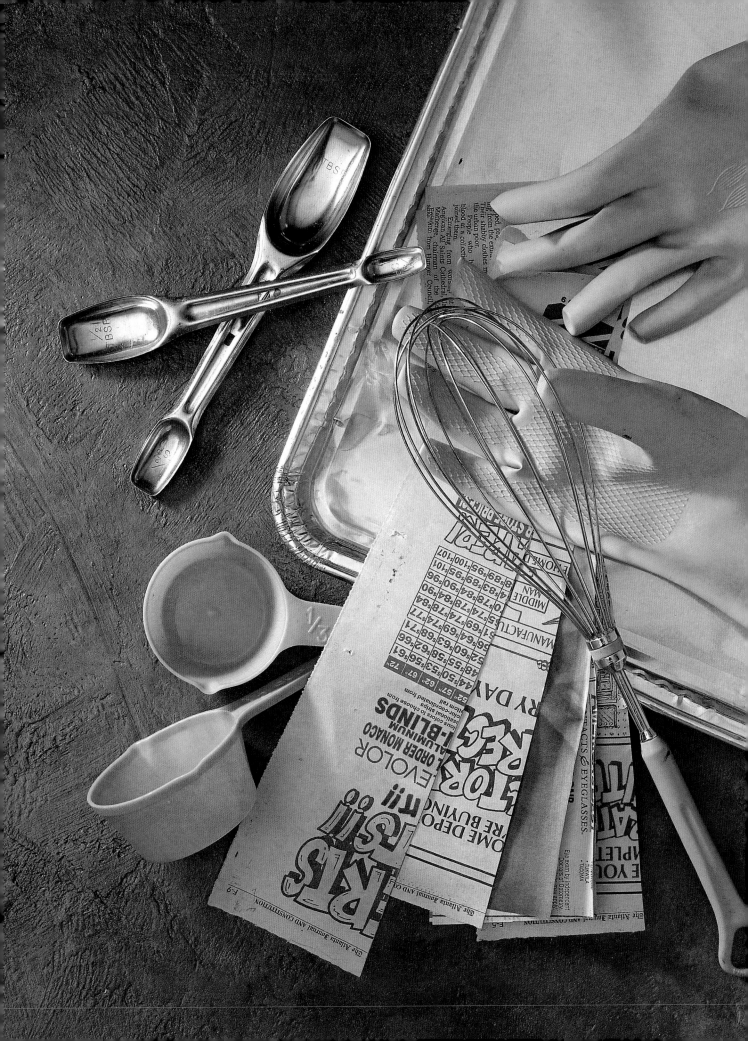

Basics

I HAVE BEEN marbling for many years, and although my work space, tools, and approach to the art form itself has evolved and changed, one thing remains constant—my love of sharing it with others. Reflecting on my marbling career always brings to light a favorite memory of mine. It comes from my very first marbling demonstration.

During the annual art fair at my son's school, volunteers demonstrated arts and crafts to each grade. I'm not sure who learned more: me or the audience.

The children's reactions were wonderful. The kindergartners and first-graders responded with "oohs" and "aaahs." The second-graders thought marbling was "Neat!" The more sophisticated third-graders agreed it was "So cool." The fourth-graders declared it "Awesome," and the fifth-graders said it was "Bad." (Does that mean "good"?) They all agreed on one thing—it was magic. Many asked if it was a magic trick. A trick it's not; magical it certainly is. As I drop the colors, rake the designs, and print the fabric, I feel like a magician.

Work Space

THE IDEAL WORK space is permanent. Unfortunately, for most of us, this type of work space is just that—ideal, but simply not realistic. One of the advantages of marbling is the minimal amount of equipment and supplies required, opening up your options for a work area.

Keep in mind a few guidelines when selecting a work area. First, your work space should be indoors. Good ventilation, without a lot of air movement, is essential so you won't be bothered by any fumes from the paints or other materials. If you work outdoors, you may find bits of dust in your marbling bath. Dust and other small materials are hard to remove and will ruin the prints. Consider working in the kitchen, basement, garage, or utility room. (If you decide to work in the kitchen, do clean carefully after marbling, and never reuse marbling equipment for cooking.)

Second, your work space should be near a water source, preferably a sink. Marbling can be messy, so cover your good countertop and flooring with a plastic drop cloth or old shower-curtain liner. If you have a water source and a tile or concrete floor in your garage or utility room, you have a great work area.

Third, an area for hanging fabric is handy, although not absolutely essential.

Lastly, we all work best and enjoy ourselves most when we're comfortable. If

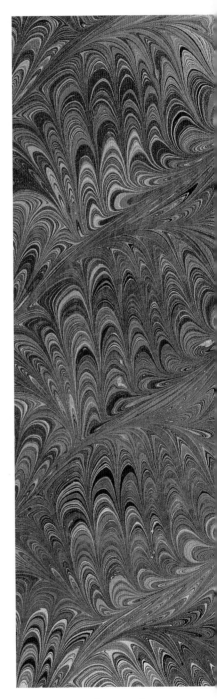

Winged Nonpareil patterned fabric

possible, adjust your worktable so you don't strain your back by bending a lot. Place thick rubber mats (available at home-improvement stores) around your work space. Wear old, comfortable clothes and sneakers with good support.

Materials

TO ORDER MARBLING supplies, contact the companies listed in "Resources" on page 92.

Alum: For the fabric's surface to hold color, you must pretreat the fabric with a mordant. A mordant is a reagent used to fix the coloring agent in textiles, leather, and other materials. The mordant used for marbling is alum. There are several kinds of alum, the most common being potassium aluminum sulfate.

For a good-quality print, you must use the right amount of alum. Using either too little or too much alum creates a pale print. If you use too little alum, the paint won't bond with the fabric. Too much alum, on the other hand, creates a barrier between the paint and the fabric surface and also prevents the paint from bonding with the fabric.

Ammonia: You will need clear household ammonia, available at grocery stores, to thicken the marbling base. Do not use ammonia products that contain colors, perfumes, detergents, surfactants, or alcohol. These added ingredients can affect the surface tension of the base.

Colorless extender: Think of colorless extender as a transparent, colorless paint that creates spaces or holes in the pattern. Use it when you want the color or print of your fabric to show through the marbled print.

Distilled water: If your tap water is hard, use distilled water for the marbling base and for thinning the marbling colors. Distilled water can be purchased at grocery stores. You can also use a water softener for hard water.

An under-alummed print

Ho-hum fabrics become exciting when marbled with colorless extender.

Fabrics: Choosing fabric for marbling is great fun. This is a great opportunity to be creative and to try unusual fabrics. Experiment with hand-painted fabrics, prints, homespuns, tissue lamé, and Ultra Suede. Look through your stash for ho-hum fabrics you can liven up.

Think of marbling as a printing process. When you choose fabric, always check the surface texture. Fabrics—natural or synthetics—with a smooth surface and tight weave provide the best prints.

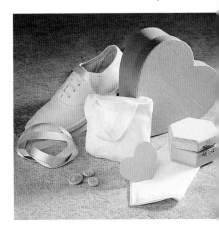

Try marbling other surfaces.

If you plan to use your marbled fabric in quilts, choose a tightly woven cotton with a high thread count, such as Pima cotton or muslin used for image-transfer processes. Remember that tightly woven fabrics are harder to hand quilt, so you may want to machine quilt your pieces as described on page 91.

If you plan to use your marbled fabric in garments, choose any tightly woven fabric with a smooth surface. Satin, polyester, polyester blends, chintz, percale, batiste, rayon, and silk—particularly China silk, silk Charmeuse, and crepe de Chine—provide outstanding results. For subtle prints, choose organza, organdy, chiffon, or tightly woven gauze fabrics.

Once you have a little experience, try marbling the fabrics in "Variations and Experiments" on pages 47–57.

Avoid fabrics with uneven surface texture or a coarse, loose weave. Silk noil, silk douppioni, silk shantung, linen, and napped fabrics, such as velveteen and corduroy, marble poorly.

To get started, you may want to go through your stash and cut an 8" x 8" square from each fabric. Be sure to include your experiments in a notebook, as described on page 15.

Because you print on the surface of the material, rather than trying to color the fibers, marbling is also a great technique for patterning items such as ribbon, canvas bags and sneakers, silk scarves, T-shirts, handkerchiefs, socks, satin balls for Christmas trees, wood and paper boxes, wooden buttons, and picture frames. Most items that absorb alum and have a slick surface will work.

Fabrics with a smooth surface, such as this China silk, marble well.

Fabrics such as linen and silk noil have an uneven texture and marble poorly.

Liquid resists: Resists stop the flow of paint from one area to another and are used when a specific shape is desired. There are several types of resists, including wax and gutta serti, which are removed by dry cleaning. For the projects in this book, I recommend using a clear or colored water-soluble resist.

Some of the more popular resists include Sabra silk resist, a colorless resist made by PRO Chemical that works well for both silk and cotton; Presist, made by Cerulean Blue; and Deka silk resist, available in clear, metallics, and many colors. Colored resist may change the feel of the fabric. G & S Dye offers a water-soluble resist that you can color with dyes (a technique you can also use for PRO Chemical & Dye's Sabra silk resist). All of these resists come with their own applicator bottle.

Marbling colors: A workable amount of colors to start with for marbling would be the three primary colors, plus white, black, and brown. I also recommend purchasing turquoise and fuchsia because these colors are difficult to mix. Colorless extender is required for many of the ideas and projects in this book. You can order wonderful premixed, easy-to-use marbling colors from PRO Chemical & Dye (see "Resources on page 92). PRO Chemical's marbling colors come in a wide range, including fluorescent colors, and are sold in convenient, needle-tip applicator bottles. You can also use Deka textile paint and silk-screen ink; Createx and Versatex airbrush inks; and Lumiére, Jacquard, and Pebeo textile paints. Most are available in a wide range of colors, including metallic, pearlescent, and fluorescent colors.

It's important to find a paint that works for you. I use many different paints, and I'm constantly looking for new paint to try. Experiment with different ones to find your favorite. (It's nice to have a variety for different effects.) A few hints: airbrush inks are more finely ground than textile paints and provide clear, crisp prints. Lumiére has the most luscious metallic paints (especially nice for stamping on marbled fabric). Pebeo marbling colors include applicator bottles and produce wonderfully crisp prints.

Textile paints or pigments, unlike fiber-reactive dyes, attach themselves to the fabric surface. (Fiber-reactive dyes chemically bond with the fibers of natural fabrics.) Textile paints have an additional adhesive or binder that helps them bond to the fabric. You can use other types of paints, but you will need to add a textile medium to make them permanent.

Textile paints provide either transparent or opaque coverage. If you use opaque paints, you will not be able to see the color of the background fabric (assuming you aren't using colorless extender). If you use transparent paints, the final colors will be based on the colors in the background fabric and the colors in your print. For example, if you use a transparent yellow paint on red fabric, your finished print will have an orange cast. You can use transparent and opaque paints together, or combine both or either with colorless extender.

You will almost certainly want to mix paint colors, as described on pages 20–23. For best results, mix the same brand of paints. (Depending on the brand, paints float and spread differently. This is a general rule, but I do mix brands when necessary.)

You may want to purchase different brands in the same colors and experiment to find which brand works best for you.

Methyl cellulose: The marbling base, or size, is the thickened water that supports the paints. There are several products used to make the marbling base; the best for fabric is methyl cellulose. I recommend PRO Chemical & Dye's methyl cellulose M112. It's safe, easy to use, and lasts longer in the tray than its popular counterpart, carrageenan.

Notebook: Keep a notebook of your experiments. Describe the paints (how each drops, covers the fabric, looks, and feels), process, and pattern. Glue or tape fabric samples into your notebook before and after printing. Be sure to record each new technique.

Surfactants: Marbling base has surface tension that affects the way paints spread. A surfactant is a liquid that, when added to your paints, helps the paints spread better. You can order a surfactant from one of the marbling suppliers or dye companies found in "Resources" on page 92. I recommend PRO Chemical's Synthrapol, which is not sold as a surfactant but works wonderfully as one, as well as being inexpensive and easy to obtain.

Use just one drop to about ½ cup paint to make your paints float and spread easier. You can also add Synthrapol to colorless extender when you want it to be more aggressive and open up larger areas on the paint.

A word of caution: make sure to use just one drop, mix well, then drop the paint on the base. One drop usually solves the problem; two drops can make the paint too aggressive; that is, the paint may spread too much and prevent other colors from spreading.

You may also want to try Kodak Photo-Flo 200, an effective surfactant chemical used by photographers. Look for Photo-Flo at photography-supply stores.

Stickers and adhesive materials: For a quick and easy resist print (see page 51), you can use children's stickers, self-adhesive reinforcements for loose-leaf-paper holes, adhesive shelf paper such as Con-Tact paper, masking tape in different widths, and PeelnStick adhesive.

Rakes and combs

Tools

YOU CAN ORDER marbling equipment from the companies listed in "Resources" on page 92, or come up with your own. Don't be afraid to be creative; there are many household items you can use for marbling.

Buckets: You will need three buckets: one for alum, one for making the marbling base, and one for holding rinse water. It's easier to manage a bucket with a handle. If you plan to work with large trays (which require many gallons of base), be sure to purchase several extra-large buckets and whisks. To speed up the mixing process, mix two batches simultaneously.

Fabric clamps: Cut 2 pieces of balsa wood, each ¼" thick and 1" wide by a little less than the width of the tray. Use the wood strips and clip-type clothespins to help lower large pieces of fabric onto the marbling base as shown on page 28.

Measuring tools: You will need measuring cups and spoons to prepare the basic recipes and mix the marbling base.

Metal whisk: Use this handy kitchen tool to mix the marbling base.

Newspaper: You will need strips of newspaper to skim or clean the marbling base before and after printing. Cut newspaper strips approximately 2" wide by the width of the tray. I like to cut lots so I have enough for many marbling sessions. A paper cutter makes the job go quickly.

Rakes and combs: Although you can create wonderful marbled patterns with a stylus, you will need rakes and combs to create complex designs. There are a few basic guidelines:

- ◆ Use waterproof materials, or apply a waterproof sealant before using.
- ◆ Try to match your rake or comb size to your tray size. You can use a too-large rake as described on page 84, but a too-small one can distort the pattern.
- ◆ Rakes and combs should be comfortable to handle.

You can purchase rakes and combs from the marbling suppliers listed on page 92, or make them, following the directions on pages 84–86.

Rubber gloves: Wear rubber gloves to protect your hands from alum, which can irritate your skin, and paints, which can temporarily change your skin color!

Stamps: Stamping is a way of applying paints and thickened dyes to the surface of fabric. Stamps work well, giving an already beautiful fabric extra dimension. You can purchase stamps at craft- and art-supply stores or make your own.

Look around the house for a variety of stamping possibilities. A crumpled paper towel or leaves from the backyard make interesting stamps for printing. You can also carve your own out of potatoes or erasers, or use glue to draw patterns on cardboard. Stamps for fabric should have large areas for holding paint and a limited amount of detail (lines don't always print clearly on fabric).

Stylus: In marbling, you use a stylus to swirl the paint drops into beautiful free-form designs. Experiment with things you find around the house. Try an old knitting needle, cocktail toothpick, wooden skewer, wide-pick comb, dowel, chopstick, skinny straw, and so on.

Tools for dropping paints: Choose from broom-corn whisks, eyedroppers, fine-line applicator bottles, plastic spoons, or straws, as described below.

♦ **Broom-corn whisks:** Broom-corn whisks are wonderful tools for dropping paint onto the marbling base. They pick up a lot of paint; just be sure to drop it in small drops. They're also easy to clean (always a big advantage).

To make broom-corn whisks, follow the instructions on page 87. They're a little time-consuming to make, but they last for years with proper care. (I've had mine for more than six years.) The cheapest way to make these is to order broom corn from a marbling supplier; if you want just a few, buy a corn broom and take it apart.

♦ **Eyedroppers:** These are a great tool for applying paint to a specific area in a design. If paint becomes clogged inside the eyedropper, remove the rubber top and use the tip of a cotton swab to clean the inside.

♦ **Fine-line applicator bottles:** Many marbling colors are sold in these bottles, and you can always refill them with paint. You can also find these in art-supply stores and through the resources on page 92.

♦ **Plastic spoons:** You can also use small plastic spoons to drop paints onto the marbling base.

♦ **Straws:** Plastic straws are an inexpensive way to apply your paints. To use, simply lower the straw into the paint, create a vacuum by placing your finger over the other end of the straw, then drop the paint onto your marbling base by removing your finger. Do not reuse straws for other colors or marbling projects.

Trays: You will probably want a variety of marbling trays. There are several criteria for good marbling trays, but the most important is that the tray be waterproof. Also, try to find one that is white or light-colored. The light color makes it easier to see the paints and patterns.

Marbling trays should be 3" to 5" deep and slightly larger than the piece of fabric you want to marble. The tray should be deep enough to accommodate a rake, but shallow enough that you don't have to mix an excessive amount of marbling base. If you're using a stylus for free-form marbling, you can use a shallower tray.

Generally speaking, the larger the tray, the less control you have. If you're new to marbling, I recommend that you start with a small tray, then work up to a larger tray.

New kitty-litter pans are a perfect beginning tray. They hold approximately three gallons of marbling base, enough for a small piece of fabric. You can also use aluminum-foil pans, photo-developing trays, and seed trays from a garden center. To make your own marbling trays, see pages 87–89.

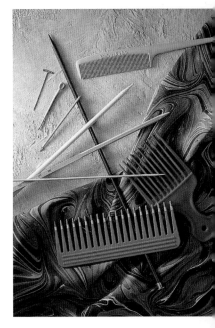

Stylus ideas

Broom-corn whisks

Handkerchiefs and napkins can be marbled in smaller trays.

For larger pieces of fabric, such as the silk crepe de Chine shown below, left, you will need larger trays. Look for cement-mixing trays and large appliance trays (for use under the washing machine) at building-supply stores, and large baking trays at a restaurant-supply store.

Recipes

MARBLING IS REALLY a two-step process. You will need to prepare the following basic recipes, soak the fabric in alum, allow the fabric to dry, and prepare the marbling base (step 1) before you begin the step-by-step process of marbling (step 2).

PREWASHING THE FABRIC

BECAUSE THE MARBLING pigments bond to the fabric surface, rather than with the fabric fibers, finishes on fabric don't usually affect marbling. Nevertheless, it's a good idea to prewash fabric (except silk). To prewash fabric, fill a washing machine with warm water and mild detergent, then wash on gentle cycle. Dry fabric on the recommended heat cycle before preparing it with alum. Remove any loose, long threads before marbling.

PRETREATING THE FABRIC

PRETREAT FABRIC WITH alum shortly before marbling, preferably no longer than 3 to 4 days in advance. If you have to leave it for longer than 4 days, wash the fabric to remove the alum, then retreat it later.

Note: The following is based on PRO Chemical & Dye's recipe for preparing an alum bath. If you use a different product, follow the manufacturer's instructions for mixing the alum bath. Proportions can vary between ¼ and ½ cup of alum to 1 gallon of water.

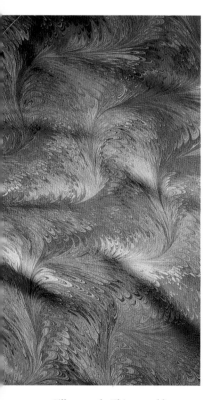

Silk crepe de Chine marbles beautifully.

You Will Need

- ¼ cup alum (see note above)
- 1 gallon water
- 3 to 5 yds. of prewashed and dried fabric in a variety of colors, prints, and fibers (It's easier to alum large pieces, then cut to size before marbling.)
- 5-gallon plastic bucket
- Clothesline
- Clothespins
- Iron and ironing board
- Long-handled spoon or whisk
- Measuring cups
- Newspaper or plastic drop cloth

- ◆ Plastic wrap
- ◆ Rubber gloves (optional)

Preparing the Alum Bath and Soaking the Fabric

1. Fill the bucket with 1 gallon of warm water (about 120° F).

2. Add the alum to the water. Stir to thoroughly dissolve the alum.

3. Place the washed and dried fabric into the alum bath. The fabric should move freely.

4. Soak the fabric for 15 to 30 minutes, stirring occasionally. Thinner fabrics need less time than thicker ones. While the fabric is soaking, suspend a clothesline over newspaper or a plastic drop cloth.

5. Remove the fabric from the bucket, gently squeezing the excess solution into the bucket.

6. Using clothespins, hang the fabric on the clothesline to drip-dry. Hang the fabric so that no part touches itself. (Where fabric touches itself, the alum becomes more concentrated, which can cause a weak or pale print.) *Do not use a clothes dryer to dry alum-soaked fabric. The heat will tenderize the fabric.*

7. After the fabric has dried, use a dry iron to remove wrinkles. Be careful; steam and water drops will remove alum and create a blotchy print!

   Cover the alum bath with plastic wrap and store for future use. Stir well before reusing. I usually keep an alum bath for 3 to 4 weeks.

PREPARING THE MARBLING BASE

FOR BEST RESULTS and to avoid air bubbles in your pattern, prepare the marbling base at least 12 hours before using. You may want to prepare and fill your tray on your worktable. Large amounts are difficult to move! If you're working with a large tray, prepare 2 buckets at a time. This recipe makes 1 gallon, which will fill a small baking tray. (A kitty litter pan holds 2 to 3 gallons.) Double or triple the recipe as needed.

You Will Need
- ◆ 1 gallon water
- ◆ 1 teaspoon clear household ammonia
- ◆ 3½ tablespoons PRO Chemical & Dye methyl cellulose M112 powder
- ◆ 5-gallon plastic bucket
- ◆ Large metal whisk
- ◆ Marbling tray
- ◆ Measuring cups and spoons
- ◆ Plastic wrap
- ◆ Rubber gloves (optional)

Hint

Make an extra gallon of marbling base and use it to replenish the solution in your tray as you marble.

Making the Base

1. Fill a bucket with 1 gallon of lukewarm water (75° to 95° F). Hot water prevents the methyl cellulose powder from dispersing.

2. Using a large metal whisk, gradually add the 3½ tablespoons of methyl cellulose to the water, stirring constantly. Add the powder slowly; stir for at least 4 minutes. Do not skimp on your stirring; cutting corners can result in a lumpy solution.

3. Add 1 teaspoon of household ammonia to the water and methyl-cellulose solution. Stir for at least 4 minutes. The solution will begin to thicken.

4. Carefully pour the marbling base into the tray. Cover with plastic wrap until you're ready to marble.

MIXING MARBLING COLORS

THE SCARIEST PART of marbling can be choosing and mixing colors. To help, I've included a few simple guidelines. Consider the following questions as you choose and look at your paint. You may want to read some of the books listed in "Further Reading" on page 93.

• **How will the final color on the fabric differ from the original color in the container?** One of the biggest advantages of working with textile paints is that what you see is what you get. For the most part, the final print color will be the same color, value, and intensity as the color you drop onto the marbling base.

• **What basic color does this color derive from?** For example, yellow-green falls between yellow and green on the color wheel.

• **What is the value of the color: light, medium, or dark?** To mix lighter values, pastels or tints, you need to add white. To mix darker values, or shades, you need to add black. Black is so strong, you only need a little to darken a color. If you were to add color to black, you would wind up with too much paint. White is the opposite. It's much easier to start with white and add drops of color until you get the desired tint.

• **What is the intensity of the color?** Is it bright or dull? To dull a color, add gray or the color's complement—the color directly opposite on the color wheel. For example, adding a small amount of blue-violet to yellow-orange will dull the color.

To start, choose three to four colors in a variety of values (see page 23). Be sure to include all the values. For example, if you have mostly medium values, be sure to also include a dark and light value.

As you become more comfortable, add more marbling colors. I use as many as eight colors per print.

A variety of values adds interest.

For students who aren't comfortable with their color sense, I recommend they choose a fabric they love, then match marbling colors to the fabric colors. I use this technique a lot when I make garments. For example, look at the vest and lining at right. I mixed marbling colors that complemented the colors in the wonderful tapestry fabric.

I wanted to emphasize the light green and dusty rose colors in the fabric, which meant I needed to mix those colors. This green leans toward blue on the color wheel; the dusty rose leans toward purple. Both colors are lighter values that appear muted or toned.

Choose marbling colors that complement another fabric.

Like mixing any recipe, there are basically two approaches. You can use a set of measuring spoons and record the quantities and results in a notebook, or you can mix by feel until you have what you want. If you don't have a lot of experience mixing colors, you may want to record your experiments. This approach makes it much easier to repeat your successes and avoid your mistakes!

For those of us who almost never follow a recipe or have no desire to carefully measure and mix colors, I've included a description of my steps for mixing dusty rose.

You Will Need

- Measuring spoons
- Plastic spoons or stirrers for mixing
- Plastic yogurt containers or baby-food jars (When you're done, replace the lids and store.)
- Synthrapol (see page 15)
- Textile paints (In this example, you will need red, violet, white, and gray or yellow-green.)
- Rubber gloves (optional)
- Water

Mixing Dusty Rose

Keep the fabric you're matching next to you and use it as a reference as you mix.

1. Start with ½ cup red; add violet or purple to make red-violet. Add 2 to 3 drops at a time until you get the desired color.

2. Add drops of red-violet to white. Add 2 drops at a time until you reach the desired tint.

3. If necessary, add drops of red or purple.

4. Add gray or yellow-green to tone down the color. The complement of red is green; the complement of red-violet is yellow-green. Both will tone down their opposites.

Now it's your turn. Mix each marbling color to the consistency of whole milk. (Thin with water if necessary.) Use a separate container and applicator for each color.

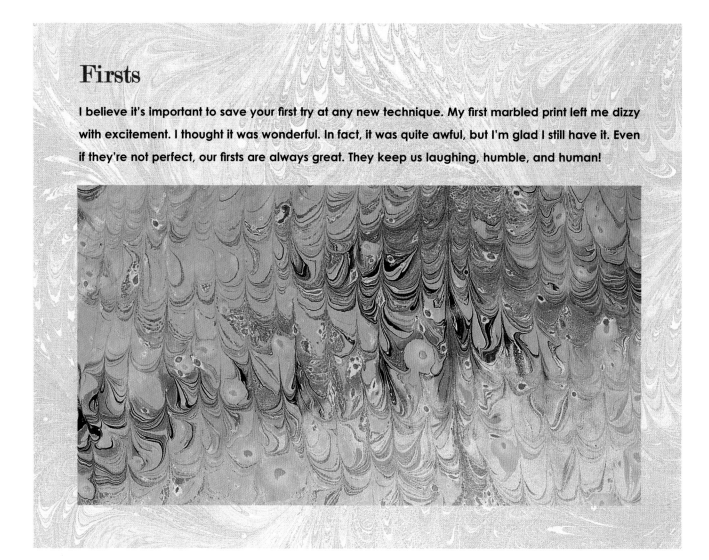

Firsts

I believe it's important to save your first try at any new technique. My first marbled print left me dizzy with excitement. I thought it was wonderful. In fact, it was quite awful, but I'm glad I still have it. Even if they're not perfect, our firsts are always great. They keep us laughing, humble, and human!

Understanding Color

In teaching, I've found that many of my students feel uncomfortable with color theory and color mixing. It really is easy, once you understand the basics.

PRIMARY COLORS: Primary colors are the three colors from which all other colors are made: red, blue, and yellow.

SECONDARY COLORS: Mixing two primary colors makes a secondary color; orange, mixed from red and yellow, is a secondary color.

TERTIARY COLORS: The colors between a primary and a secondary color on the color wheel are tertiary colors. These are made by mixing a primary and a secondary color; yellow-green is made by mixing yellow and green.

COMPLEMENTARY COLOR SCHEME: A complementary color scheme uses two colors on opposite sides of the color wheel. You can use one primary and one secondary color, such as red and green, or two tertiary colors, such as red-violet and yellow-green.

MONOCHROMATIC COLOR SCHEME: A monochromatic color scheme uses only the shades and tints of one color.

ANALOGOUS COLOR SCHEME: An analogous color scheme uses colors next to each other on the color wheel, and includes at least one tertiary color. For example, an analogous color scheme could include blue, blue-green, and green.

VALUE: Value refers to the lightness or darkness of a color.

TONE: A tone is a color that has been dulled with gray.

INTENSITY: Instensity refers to the brightness or dullness of a color. Pure colors are intense; toned colors are not.

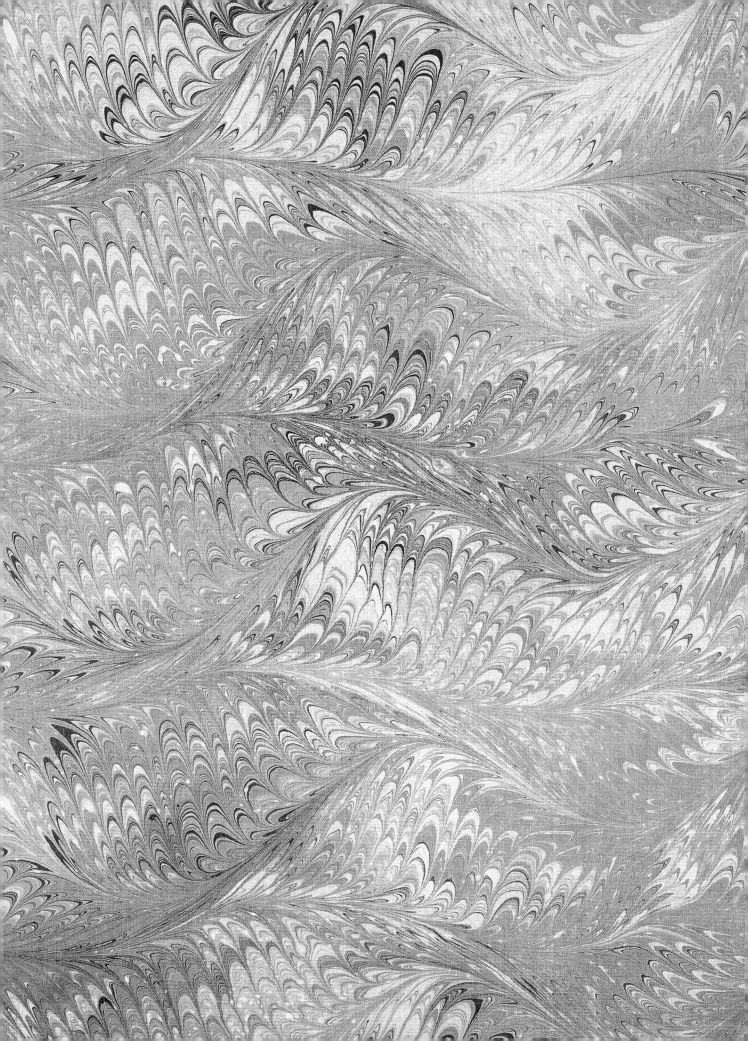

Marbling

NOW YOU'RE READY for step 2: making a print. Choose a pattern from those on pages 32–46, read the following step-by-step instructions, then let the fun begin!

You Will Need

- 5-gallon bucket
- 8" x 8" pan
- Broom-corn whisks, eyedroppers, and/or needle-tip applicator bottles (1 for each marbling color)
- Clothesline
- Clothespins
- Colorless extender (optional)
- Extra marbling base
- Fabric, pretreated in alum bath (see page 18) and cut to fit within your marbling tray
- Funnel (optional)
- Marbling base in tray (see page 19)
- Marbling colors, at least 4
- Newspaper, cut into 2"-wide strips
- Plastic drop cloth(s)
- Plastic wrap
- Rakes, combs, and/or stylus appropriate for your chosen pattern (To make the Waved Icarus pattern shown in the following steps, you will need 1" and 3" rakes and any size nonpareil comb.)
- Rubber gloves (optional)
- Scissors for trimming fabric threads
- Sticks for lowering fabric
- Synthrapol, or another marbling surfactant (see page 15)
- Water

Preparing Your Work Space

SET UP YOUR work space close to a water source if possible.

1. Cover your worktable with a plastic drop cloth. Gather your tools and materials.

2. Place the prepared marbling base on the table if necessary.

Hint

Don't feel that you have to rush through the marbling steps, but do work fairly quickly. Marbling colors that are left on the base too long may begin to separate, making it difficult to create a quality print.

Use newspaper strips to skim the base.

3. Fill the 5-gallon bucket with lukewarm water. This will be your rinse bucket.

4. Hang a clothesline nearby, and cover the floor underneath with a plastic drop cloth.

Skimming the Marbling Base

BEFORE YOU MAKE a print, always remove air bubbles, dust, leftover paint, etc. from the surface of the marbling base.

1. Hold a strip of newspaper at a slight angle as shown, just touching the surface of the marbling base.

2. Beginning at one end of the tray, pull the paper toward you to skim the surface. Discard newspaper.

Dropping the Marbling Colors

THE ORDER IN which you drop the marbling colors is a critical factor in the overall look of the print. The first color becomes thin and intense, squeezed into a fine line by the colors that follow. The last color has the most presence and is also the most diffused. You may want to experiment by using the same four paints on the same four pieces of fabric, raking each with the same design but dropping the paints in a different order.

Before you start marbling, test each color. Place 1 drop of color on the marbling base. The drop should float on the surface and gradually spread in a circle. If the drop doesn't spread, add 1 drop of Synthrapol or another surfactant and test again.

You can use an 8" x 8" pan filled with marbling base to test how colors drop. I keep a small pan near the marbling tray for this purpose.

1. Using a broom-corn whisk, eyedropper, and/or needle-tip applicator bottle, place drops of the first marbling color on the marbling base. *The tip of your applicator should never touch the surface of the base.* Hold the applicator 3" to 12" above the surface; find the height that works best for you.

2. Repeat step 1 for the remaining colors (and colorless extender if desired). For best results, completely cover the surface of your marbling tray with drops of color. This ensures an intense print.

Dropping paints on the marbling base. (This is called a "Stones" pattern.)

The same four fabrics marbled with the same four colors in the same design look different because the colors were dropped in a different order.

You may want to vary the tools as you drop colors. The whisk provides lots of drops for good coverage. The eyedropper and applicator bottle give you more control over placement.

Raking the Marbling Pattern

REFERRING TO PAGES 32–46, follow the illustrations for your desired pattern. In the following steps, I used my favorite, the Waved Icarus.

1. Push a 1" rake along the length of the tray, away from you. Hold the rake or comb at a slight angle (bottom toward you). The angle helps create a better print because there is less drag on the paint. The bottom of the rake should always be angled opposite the direction you're raking.

2. Pick up the rake, move it over, then bring it toward you, parallel to the previous lines.

3. Working right to left, draw the 1" rake across the tray.

4. Working left to right and between the previous lines, draw the 1" rake across the tray.

5. Working from the top of the tray, pull the ½" comb toward you.

6. Working from right to left, pull the 3" rake across the tray, using a wavelike motion.

Step 1

Step 2

Step 3

Step 4

Step 5

Step 6

Step 2 of Making a Print

Step 4 of Making a Print

Step 5 of Making a Print

Step 1 of Rinsing the Fabric

Making a Print

1. Clamp the fabric to the balsa-wood sticks with clothespins.

2. Referring to the photo, hold the sticks so the fabric forms a **U**-shape above the tray. Lower the bottom of the **U** onto the paints; then gently lower the sides.

3. Remove the clothespins and sticks.

4. Lay strips of newspaper around the edges of the fabric. Most of the color will be picked up by the fabric during the printing process. This step is optional, but it makes cleanup much easier.

5. When the back side of the fabric appears wet, remove the fabric. (The fabric prints instantly, but to play it safe, I wait about 1 minute before removing the fabric from the tray.) Pick up the fabric at the corners. Using the other hand, gently squeeze excess paint and base into the marbling tray.

Rinsing the Fabric

1. Gently rinse the fabric in the rinse bucket. If you prefer, you can also rinse the fabric under a gently running tap. Rinse until the water is clear.

    You can put several prints in the rinse bucket at one time, then rinse at the same time.

2. Remove the fabric from the bucket and gently squeeze to remove excess water.

3. Using clothespins, hang the fabric on the clothesline to dry.

4. Allow the fabric to cure for several days. Refer to the manufacturer's instructions for setting the textile paints. Use a pressing cloth for fabrics with a low heat tolerance, such as silk.

Cleaning Up

1. Skim the surface of the marbling base with a strip of newspaper as described above. If you plan to marble again soon, cover the marbling base and colors with plastic wrap or airtight lids. The base may look murky, but it's usually good for more than one session.

2. Rinse the marbling tools in lukewarm water. Do not use soap; soap residue on tools can create contaminated prints.

3. Empty the tray in a sink. Rinse thoroughly. Remember, do not use soap.

Troubleshooting

A GOOD-QUALITY print should have a clear, even color and pattern. While lack of experience can affect the quality of your print (look at my first print on page 22), more often the problem is caused by something else. As with any form of surface design, things can and do go wrong. Don't be discouraged! Disappointing prints are great candidates for shadow marbling (see page 50). Following are some of the problems you may encounter.

The marbling colors sink to the bottom of the tray.
 •   The marbling base may be too thick. Thin the marbling base with water. You will need to experiment. Start with ½ cup water for 3 gallons of marbling base. Skim, then reapply marbling colors.
 •   The marbling colors may be too thick. Thin the colors with water, skim the marbling base, then test. You may need to add a surfactant, such as Synthrapol, to the marbling colors. The surfactant increases the color's ability to float and spread.

The marbling colors spread too much.
 •   You may have added too much surfactant or water to the marbling color. Add more paint.
 •   The marbling base may be too thin or old. Add 1 teaspoon methyl powder per gallon of solution, or discard and make a new recipe.

The marbling colors appear grainy.
 •   The pigments in the textile paints have separated. Remix paints thoroughly.
 •   The textile paints may be too old. Purchase new paints.

The marbling colors floating on the base have jagged edges.
 •   This is caused by a skin forming on the surface of the marbling base, much like a skin forms on pudding or custard. Thoroughly skim your marbling base before each use.

The marbling color expands, then immediately contracts.
 •   The marbling *base* is too cold. Warm to room temperature, then reapply marbling colors.
 •   The marbling *color* is too cold. Warm to room temperature, then reapply to marbling base.

The marbled print appears fuzzy.
 •   The marbling base is too thick. Add water to the marbling base, then reapply marbling colors.
 •   The marbling colors may be too thick. Thin the colors with water, then test.
 •   There was too much time between raking the pattern and printing the fabric. Work more quickly.

Hint

Every so often, you need to add more marbling base to the tray. Always add new marbling base slowly to avoid air bubbles. I use a funnel so the new solution enters near the bottom of the tray.

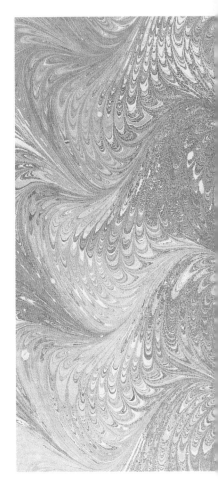

A grainy print

A contaminated print

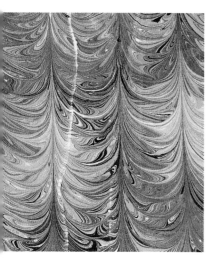

A thread caused the line on this print.

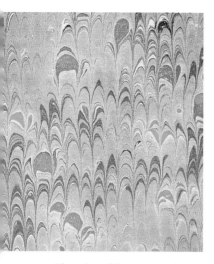

The paints did not competely expand on this distorted print.

The marbled print has lines of color that separate from each other.

♦ This is a sign of contamination. Some artists like this look and use it in their work. To avoid contamination, clean your tools with warm water before reusing or use a different set.

The marbled print has small dots or lines.

♦ Small dots or lines on a print are usually caused by dust or thread. Thoroughly skim the marbling base before each use, and be sure to remove any loose threads from the fabric.

There is a circle on the printed fabric.

♦ There was an air bubble on the surface of the marbling base. Thoroughly skim the marbling base before each use.

The printed pattern is distorted.

♦ You may have hesitated when you placed your fabric on the marbling base. Be sure to lower your fabric in one smooth motion, placing the center down first.

♦ If you do not allow the marbling colors to completely expand before raking, your print may be distorted. Allow the colors to expand before raking.

The printed pattern appears mushy.

♦ If the print lacks definition or the colors are blurred, the marbling colors were overraked. Follow the pattern instructions and avoid overraking.

The marbling colors or print wash off in the rinse.

♦ The alum bath may have been too weak or too strong. Too little alum prevents fabric from holding color. Too much alum creates a barrier on the fabric surface. Follow the recipe exactly.

The printed fabric is fragile and easily rips.

♦ Alum will begin to weaken the fabric if the treated fabric is left too long before marbling. Refer to the guidelines on page 18.

A mushy print

Choosing a Pattern

THE MARBLING PATTERNS in this book are not exact replicas of traditional marbling designs; they've been modified to work on fabric. All of the patterns are based on either a Get-gel or a Nonpareil marbling design. To make it easier for you to find and follow the desired pattern, I've grouped each pattern alphabetically by type: Get-gel or Nonpareil. As you gain experience, you'll begin to recognize the base pattern of different marbling designs. Note that each type has the same basic steps.

Refer to the following to understand the pattern illustrations.

- ◆ Solid lines indicate the current step. Dashed lines indicate the previous step.
- ◆ The rake or comb size, for example, 1" rake, refers to the distance between the tines.
- ◆ All marbling patterns begin with the same step: dropping the marbling colors on the base. This is actually a traditional marbling pattern, referred to as "Stones." See the photo at the bottom of page 26.
- ◆ Arrows pointing down: Pull the rake or comb from the opposite end of the tray toward you.
- ◆ Arrows pointing up: Push the rake or comb away from you toward the opposite end of the tray.
- ◆ Arrows pointing to the side: Draw the rake or comb across the tray, following the direction of the arrows.
- ◆ Curving arrows: Draw the rake, comb, or stylus in a wave or spiral motion as shown in the illustration.

Patterns can finish horizontally or vertically. For example, this book shows how to rake a vertical Get-gel pattern. If you want to rake a horizontal Get-gel, change the orientation of the pattern steps.

Free-form Marbling

Experiment with free-form designs. Use a stylus to add detail to a raked pattern or newly dropped paint.

Get-gel Marbling Designs

Angel Fish

Drop colors.

2" rake

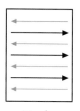

2" rake

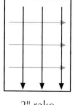

2" rake

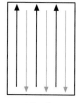

2" rake

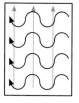

2" rake

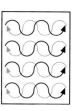

2" rake

Feathered Chevron

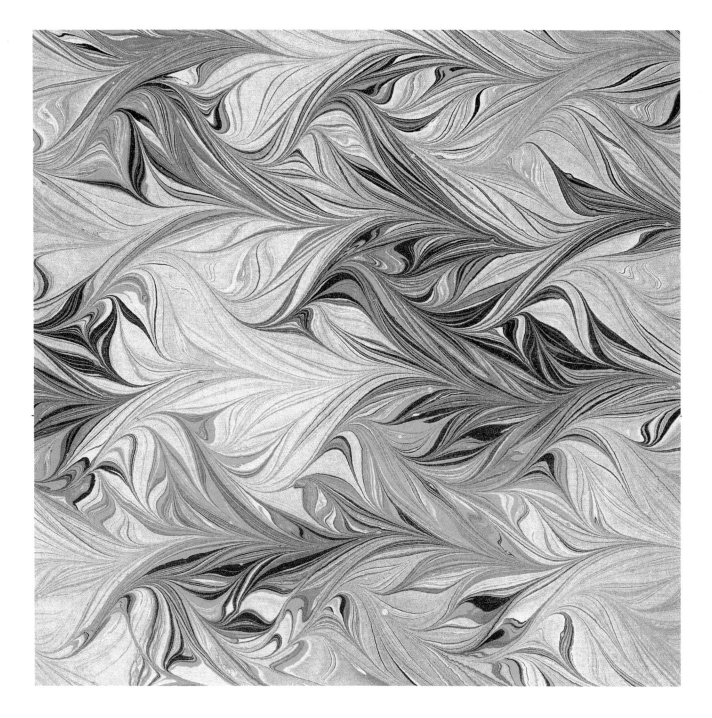

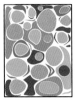

Drop colors.

1" rake

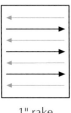

1" rake

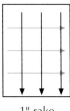

1" rake

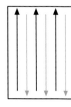

1" rake

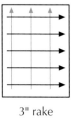

3" rake

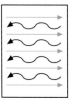

3" rake

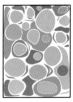

Drop colors.

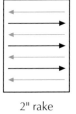

2" rake

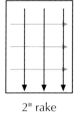

2" rake

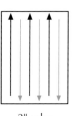

2" rake

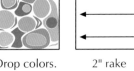

2" rake

Peacock

Drop colors.

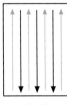

2" rake

2" rake

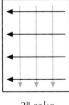

2" rake

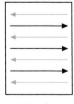

2" rake

Bouquet
comb

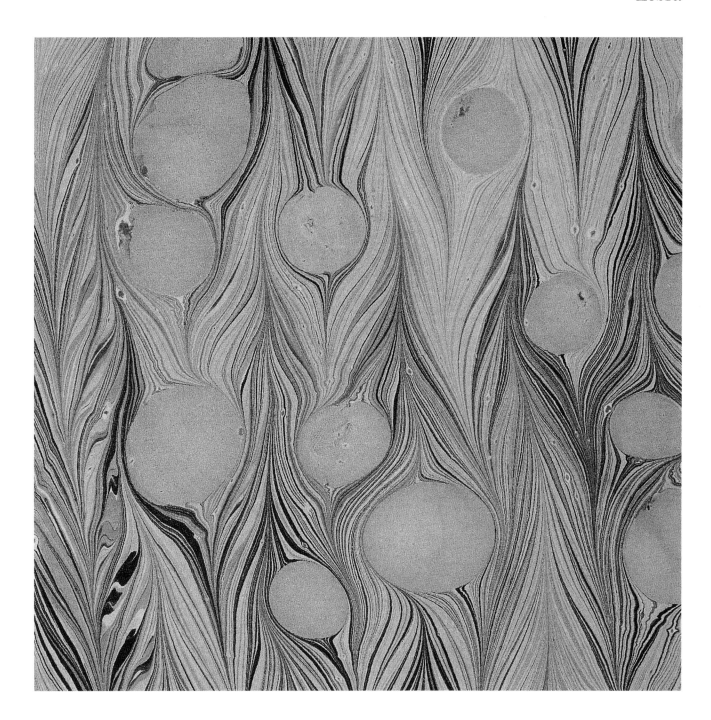

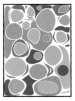

Drop colors.

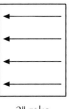

2" rake

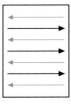

2" rake

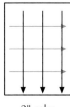

2" rake

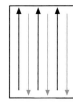

2" rake

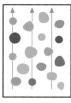

Drop colors.

Nonpareil Marbling Designs

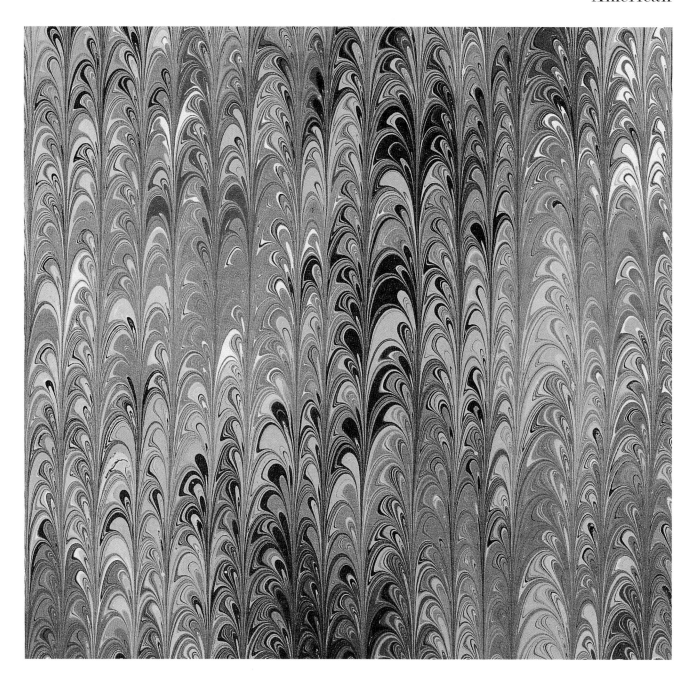

Drop colors.

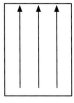

1" rake

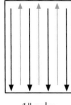

1" rake

1" rake

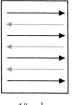

1" rake

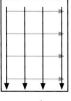

1" rake

1" rake

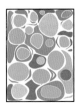

Drop colors.

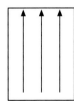

1" rake

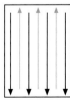

1" rake

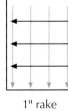

1" rake

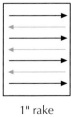

1" rake

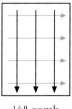

½" comb

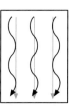

Bouquet
comb

Cascade

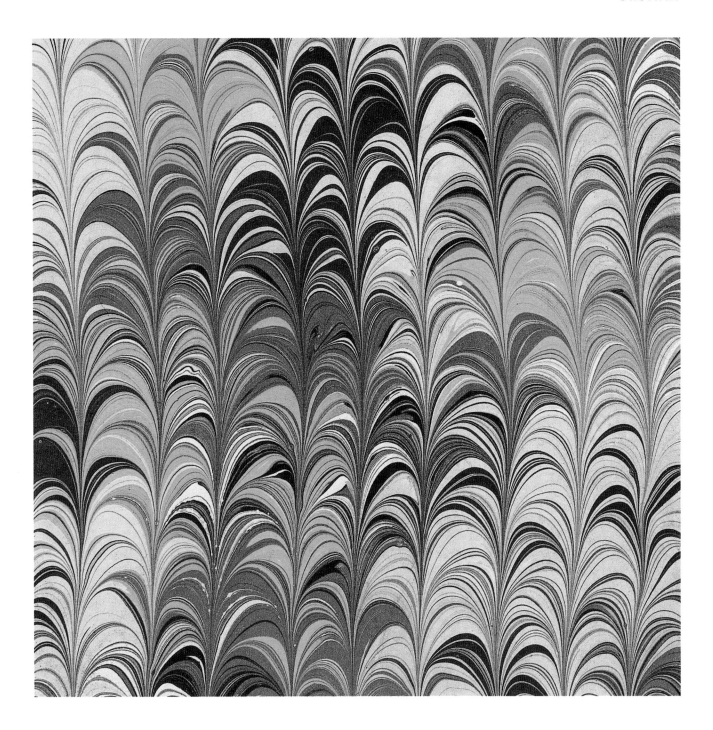

Drop colors.

1" rake

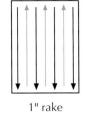

1" rake

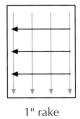

1" rake

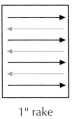

1" rake

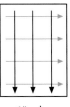

1" rake

1" rake

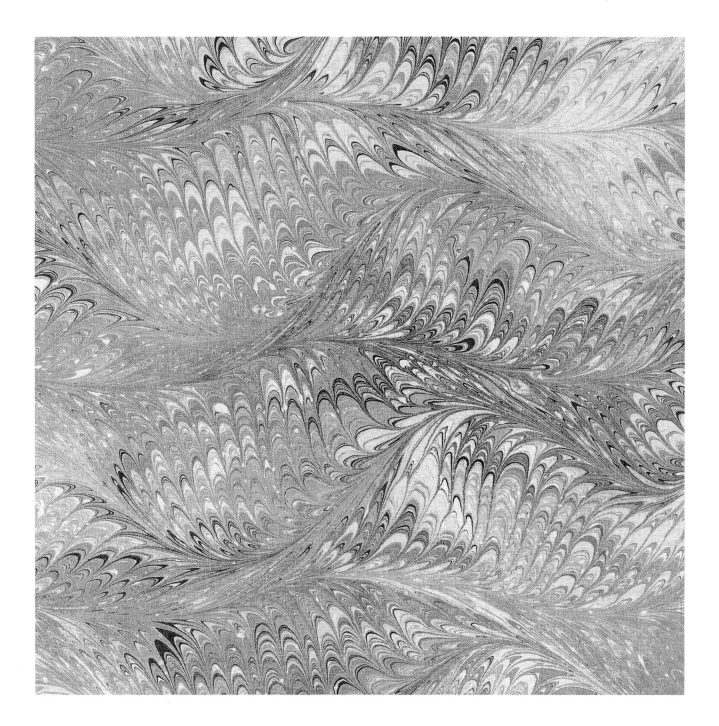

Drop colors.

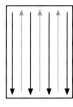
1" rake

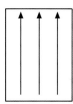
1" rake

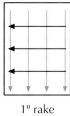
1" rake

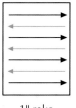
1" rake

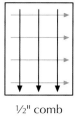
½" comb

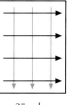
3" rake

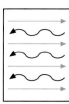
3" rake

French Curl

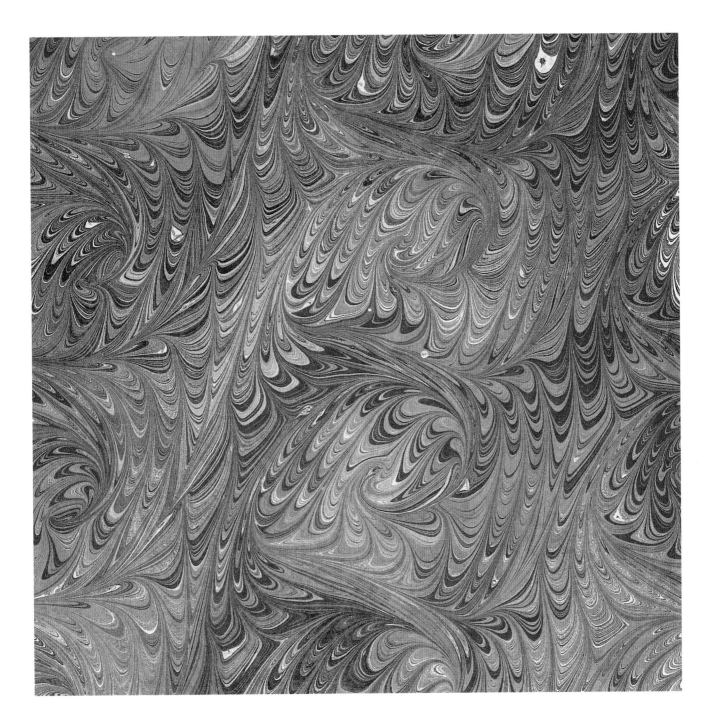

Drop colors.

1" rake

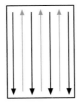

1" rake

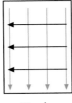

1" rake

1" rake

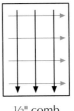

½" comb

3" rake

Drop colors.

1" rake

1" rake

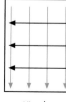
1" rake

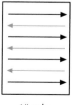
1" rake

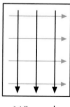
½" comb

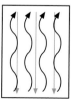
Bouquet comb

Nonpareil

Drop colors.

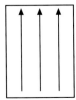

1" rake

1" rake

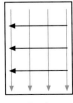

1" rake

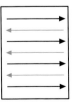

1" rake

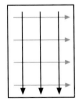

½" comb

Drop colors.

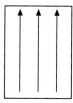

1" rake

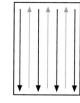

1" rake

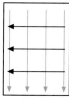

1" rake

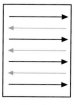

1" rake

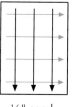

½" comb

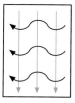

3" rake

Waved Nonpareil

Drop colors.	1" rake	1" rake	1" rake	1" rake	½" comb	3" rake

  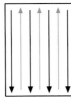 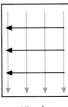 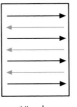 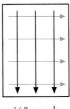 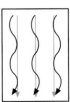

Drop colors.

1" rake

1" rake

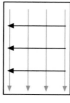

1" rake

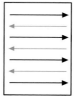

1" rake

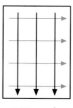

½" comb

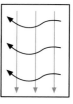

3" rake

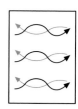

3" rake

Variations and Experiments

SHORTLY AFTER I began marbling, I started to combine other techniques with it. (I've never been able to "leave well enough alone," and marbling was no exception.) I found that by using an extensive amount of colorless extender while marbling on top of prints and hand-painted fabrics, much of the background was revealed.

I loved using both liquid and adhesive resists in the marbling process, then painting in the blank areas. A pretty, but all too subtle marbled print led me to try stamping. Marbling takes on a whole new dimension when combined with these techniques!

Using Colorless Extender

IN MARBLING, each color remains separate, but all work together to form an intricate network of color and lines. Colorless extender opens up areas in the print, allowing your fabric to show through. Compare the fabrics at right; the marbled print creates interest and dimension without hiding the wonderful background.

Marbling with a colorless extender

Dragon lining

Working with Special Fabrics

MY FIRST EXPOSURE to marbled fabric was pigment on white or natural-colored fabric. Over the years, I've discovered many other wonderful fabrics for marbling. I've also discovered that marbling can work with the background fabric as an equal component. This concept of treating marbling not as a focal point, but as an equal partner with the fabric is an exciting approach.

Because marbling is a printing process, most fibers are acceptable. With new fabrics popping up all the time, there is always something different to try. This keeps the art form fresh and exciting.

ULTRA SUEDE

ULTRA SUEDE MARBLES beautifully. To see the original suede fabric, use colorless extender with your marbling colors. One of the advantages of Ultra Suede is that you can marble both sides of the fabric. Prepare each side separately: pretreat with alum, dry, marble, and cure one side, then repeat the process for the other side. The marbling process is the same as with any other fabric, but avoid excessive squeezing in the alum bath and rinsing steps. Be sure the rinse bucket is large enough so the fabric doesn't rub against itself.

I like to use marbled Ultra Suede in garments and in appliqués like those shown below.

SHEERS

SHEER FABRICS MARBLE beautifully, but lose their transparency under the painted areas. Experiment with colorless extender for a nice contrast to the marbled pattern areas. The marbling process is the same as for any other fabric.

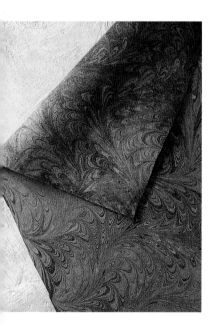

Suede can be marbled on both sides.

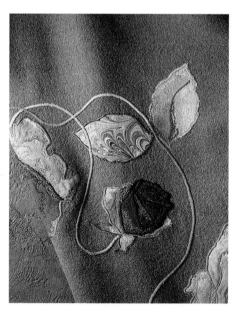

Elegant Ultra Suede appliqués

Sheer fabrics are interesting to marble.

TISSUE LAMÉ

I LOVE MARBLING tissue lamé. Although the process is tricky, the results are worth the effort.

Tissue lamé has a high metal content, so it will not readily absorb the alum. My first attempts at marbling lamé resulted in a perfect print that slid back onto the base when I held up the fabric.

After much trial and error, I came up with the following process.

You Will Need

- ◆ Alum bath (see page 18)
- ◆ Colorless extender
- ◆ Createx Additive Bond All
- ◆ Createx airbrush inks
- ◆ Createx Catalyst
- ◆ Iron and ironing board
- ◆ Marbling materials and tools (see page 25)
- ◆ Pressing cloth
- ◆ Tissue lamé

Marbling the Fabric

1. Follow the directions for "Pretreating the Fabric" on page 18, but double the amount of alum in the recipe.

2. Referring to the manufacturer's instructions, mix Createx airbrush inks with the recommended amounts of Createx Catalyst and Createx Additive Bond All. These additives help the colors adhere to the fabric surface. Use lots of colorless extender to allow the tissue lamé to show through.

3. Marble the fabric, following the steps on pages 25–28 with one exception: When it is time to remove the fabric from the tray, lift it carefully and *do not* squeeze it. Gently submerge the fabric once in a large rinse bath or tray. *The fabric should not touch itself; if it does, the paints may smear and ruin the pattern.*

4. Lay the fabric on a flat surface to dry.

5. Allow the fabric to cure, following the paint manufacturer's instructions. Before heat setting, rinse in cool water. (The first rinse process is so delicate, some of the methyl cellulose remains behind. After the print dries, you can give it this second rinse to remove any remaining methyl cellulose.)

6. Heat-set. Turn your fabric to the wrong side and cover with a pressing cloth. Iron, using a suitable setting.

While the process is a bit delicate, the cured fabric is quite sturdy. Like any delicate fabric, marbled tissue lamé should be dry-cleaned rather than machine washed.

Tissue lamé is tricky to marble, but worth the effort.

Rinse lamé carefully.

"Mistakes" are great candidates for shadow marbling.

Shadow Marbling

OVERMARBLING, OR SHADOW marbling, turns your beasts into beauties. Shadow marbling is especially effective when there is a difference in intensity or value. If both prints are light, they wash each other out; if both are dark, they overpower each other. It's best to have one light print and one dark print.

You Will Need
- Colorless extender
- Marbled fabric, pretreated with alum (see page 18)
- Marbling materials and tools (see page 25)
- Rubber gloves (optional)

Marbling the Fabric

1. Marble the pretreated fabric, following the steps on pages 25–28. Use darker or lighter values (than the previous print) and colorless extender.

2. Rinse, dry, and heat-set the fabric.

Using Resists

A RESIST PREVENTS pigment from bonding to the fabric in the marbling process. There are many unique resists and ways to use them.

Self-adhesive resists provide a quick and easy way to combine resists and marbling. They are applied to the fabric before marbling, then removed after the process. You can leave the resisted area as is, or overmarble, paint, or stamp it.

Shadow marbling can turn your beasts into beauties.

ADHESIVE RESISTS

HERE ARE A few easy-to-find items that work great as marbling resists:

- ◆ Children's stickers
- ◆ Self-adhesive reinforcements for loose-leaf-paper holes
- ◆ Adhesive shelf paper, such as Con-Tact paper
- ◆ Masking tape in different widths
- ◆ PeelnStick adhesive

Avoid stickers that have been approved for home decorating (such as walls and windows). Home-decor adhesives are less sticky, and your marbling colors may bleed under the shape. My favorite adhesive resist is PeelnStick; it provides good coverage.

For best results, choose sand-washed China silk and smooth cottons. Avoid thin fabrics; the marbling colors may seep under the adhesive resist.

You Will Need

- ◆ Adhesive material
- ◆ Fabric, pretreated in alum bath (see page 18)
- ◆ Marbling materials and tools (see page 25)
- ◆ Rubber gloves (optional)
- ◆ Scissors (if you want to cut out shapes or designs from the adhesive material)

Making a Print Using an Adhesive Resist

1. Prepare your stickers, cutting out shapes if desired.

2. Press the stickers onto the right side of the pretreated fabric.

3. Marble the prepared fabric, following the steps on pages 25–28.

4. Remove the fabric from the marbling base quickly (within about 10 seconds). If paint seems to be seeping under the adhesive, remove the fabric immediately. Remove the adhesive material after rinsing.

Resists make interesting quilt blocks.

> ### Hint
> *When using resists for a specific place on a garment, lightly trace the pattern piece on the fabric, then position the adhesive material.*

Marbled resist fabric and stickers

Marbling using a tape resist and colorless extender

Cut adhesive papers into shapes and press onto fabric.

Shadow marbling with resists

RESIST QUILT BLOCKS

MARBLED RESISTS ARE a fun way to make interesting blocks for quilts or other patchwork projects.

You Will Need
- ♦ Adhesive material (see page 15)
- ♦ Fabric, pretreated in alum bath (see page 18)
- ♦ Marbling materials and tools (see page 25)
- ♦ Scissors

Making a Quilt Block

1. Cut a piece of pretreated fabric the desired block size, including seam allowances. Fold the square in half diagonally in both directions to find the center.

2. Cut a shape from the adhesive material. Position the shape on the center of the block, using the fold lines as guides.

3. Marble the prepared fabric, following the steps on pages 25–28. Remove the adhesive material after rinsing.

    You can use the block as is, or as a center square in another block pattern.

RESISTS WITH SHADOW MARBLING

ANOTHER INTERESTING VARIATION is to marble using a resist, remove the resist, re-alum the fabric, then overmarble.

Painting Resist Areas

Experiment with coloring the resist areas after marbling. You can use dye pens, oil-stick crayons, permanent fabric markers, or textile paints. Heat-set the inks or paints, following the manufacturer's instructions.

REVERSE RESISTS

THIS VARIATION IS similar to the idea of reverse appliqué. It's fun to use on napkins, pillows, and clothing.

You Will Need

- ♦ Adhesive shelf paper (see page 15)
- ♦ Embroidery hoop
- ♦ Fabric, pretreated in alum bath (see page 18)
- ♦ Marbling materials and tools (see page 25)
- ♦ Scissors

Reverse resists

Making a Reverse Resist

1. From your adhesive shelf paper, cut out a square or rectangle that is large enough to protect the fabric around your desired shape.

2. From the center of the shelf-paper square or rectangle, cut out a shape, such as the heart shown at left. Start cutting in the middle of the shape.

3. Firmly press the shelf paper onto the pretreated fabric. Place the fabric in an embroidery hoop, centering the shape area.

4. Marble the shape, following the steps on pages 25–28. Do not allow the area to remain on the marbling base for long. The base can seep under the adhesive edges and ruin the print. Remove the adhesive material before heat setting.

Painting a Shadow-Marbled Resist Print

If there is not enough contrast between the resist shape and the surrounding area, you can make the image more prominent with feather painting.

1. After shadow marbling, reposition the adhesive shape over the resist. (You may need to cut a new adhesive shape.)

2. Using textile paint and a paintbrush, lightly feather the color around the edges of the resist shape. (Work out 1/4" to 1/2" from the shape.)

3. Remove the adhesive shapes. Dry, cure, and heat-set, following the paint manufacturer's instructions.

SILK-PAINT RESISTS

IN THIS TECHNIQUE, you use a liquid resist and silk paints to embellish a shape created by an adhesive resist. First, you apply a liquid resist around the shape (resist area), then you paint inside the shape.

Textile paints are fairly thick and do not migrate or spread out when applied to fabric. Silk paints are thinner and migrate easily.

Be sure to use a liquid resist specifically formulated for silk paints. See page 14 for different types of liquid resists.

You Will Need

+ Embroidery hoop
+ Paintbrush
+ Pigma pen (optional)
+ Silk, prepared with an adhesive resist and marbled (see page 51)
+ Silk paints
+ Silk resist, such as Deka silk resist or PRO Chemical & Dye Sabra silk resist

Painting a Resist Shape

1. Place the prepared fabric in an embroidery hoop. The hoop keeps an area elevated (off the surface) to prevent smearing.

2. Apply silk resist to the edge where the marbling meets the resist shape (created by the adhesive). Allow the silk resist to dry.

3. Using a paintbrush and silk paint, apply paint inside the resist lines, working out from the center of the shape.

4. Allow paint to dry. Heat-set, following the paint manufacturer's instructions.

5. To remove the resist, soak the fabric in water. To add definition, such as leaf veins, use a Pigma pen. Stabilize the fabric as described in the "Hint" on page 67 before drawing.

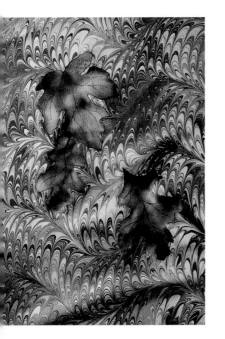

Painted resists

Step 2

Step 4

Stamping

USE STAMPS TO add dimension and interest to your marbled pieces. Stamping works especially well on fabrics with subtle prints.

Choose a stamp shape that complements your marbling pattern. For example, a curved shape, such as a leaf, works well with the Waved Icarus pattern.

You Will Need

- Marbled fabric (preferably a subtle print)
- Paintbrush, 1"
- Plastic drop cloth or newspaper
- Plastic plate, 1 for each color of paint
- Plastic spoon, 1 for each color of paint
- Stamps (see page 16)
- Textile paints (metallic paints work especially well)

Stamping the Fabric

1. Cover your worktable with a plastic drop cloth or several layers of newspaper. Place a piece of marbled fabric on the table, smoothing to remove wrinkles.

2. Using a plastic spoon, spread a small amount of paint on a plastic plate.

3. Using the paintbrush, paint the stamp surface.

4. Carefully press the stamp onto the fabric. Apply pressure evenly. (Do not rock the stamp back and forth.) You may want to make a few test prints first.

5. Allow paint to dry. Heat-set, following the paint manufacturer's instructions.

Scalloping

SCALLOPING IS AN elegant, easy technique for finishing projects made from marbled fabric. The "Soup-Can Prints" (page 72) and the "Fancy Scallops Vest" (page 74) feature this technique. (See the individual projects for step-by-step directions.)

The trick to scalloping is choosing the right marble pattern. Cascade (page 39), Nonpareil (page 43), Waved Icarus (page 44), and Winged Nonpareil (page 46) all work well because of the patterns' curves and whorls.

You can embellish almost any project with scalloping. Look at the detail on the sleeves at right. I marbled tissue lamé with a Waved Icarus pattern, then backed the lamé with fusible web and two coordinating fabrics. The edges of each layer are trimmed to mirror the marbled pattern. In this garment, the coordinating fabrics intensify the color without overwhelming the tissue lamé.

Experiment with the technique. Look at the simple scalloped "Treasure Bag" in the photo on page 61. I accentuated the scalloped edges with free-motion machine

Stamped prints

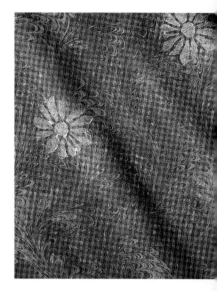

More ideas

Scalloped-edge sleeves

Choose curving patterns for scalloping.

stitching. (For more information on embellishment techniques, see "Further Reading" on page 93.)

Making a Three-Color Progression

A THREE-COLOR progression features a planned color movement in an analogous color scheme. An analogous color scheme is based on three adjacent colors on a color wheel (see page 23)—for example, green, blue-green, and blue.

Choose three adjacent colors on the color wheel. Mix several values or variations for each color. For the green shown on the facing page, I mixed three different greens: a light green, a medium blue-green, and a dark green.

You Will Need
+ Marbling materials and tools (see page 25)
+ Marbling colors, 3 colors plus 2 or 3 variations of each color

Making a Three-Color Progression

1. Choose a marbling pattern. The Nonpareil patterns work especially well with this technique.

2. Marble your fabric, following the steps on pages 25–28. Mentally divide your marbling tray in thirds. When you drop your marbling colors, drop color 1 at the top of the tray, color 2 in the middle, and color 3 at the bottom. Slightly overlap the colors.

3. Rake carefully so the three colors blend at the edges, but do not overrake.

4. Allow fabric to dry. Heat-set, following the paint manufacturer's instructions.

Three-color progression print

Gallery Show

"Where Dragons Dwell" was featured in The Fairfield Fashion Show—Diamond Extravaganza, produced by Fairfield Processing Corporation. Photo by Debbie Porter.

A marbled lining adds elegance to this embellished tapestry vest. Even though not many people will see it, knowing it's there tickles me.

Hand-dyed fabric marbled with a simple masking-tape resist creates an intriguing pillow.

Marbled homespun, scalloping, and appliqué were used to create this pretty, whimsical "Country Homespun Pillow."

Marbled fabrics provide wonderful treasure bags for gifts or your own personal treasures.

The lining art reveals the title of this fun "He Loves Me Vest."

Machine quilting on marbled fabric creates the incredible dimension in this stunning "Painted Desert Lights Jacket."

Sneakers are a fun place to show off your marbling skills.

Scalloped edging echoes the marbling pattern on this "Fancy Scallops Vest."

Marbled fabric, stamping, and couching combine to produce this striking "Falling Leaves Quilt."

Marbled fabric and stamping add movement and interest to this traditional Pinwheel quilt pattern.

Projects

Silk Scarf

A MARBLED SILK SCARF, like those on the facing page, is a lovely way to show off your accomplishment—to wear or give as a special gift. For silk scarf "blanks"— garments prepared for surface design—see "Resources" on page 92.

You Will Need
- Iron and ironing board
- Hemmed silk scarf, white or colored, pretreated in alum bath (see page 18)
- Marbling materials and tools (see page 25)
- Pilot pen, gold or silver
- Temporary stabilizer

Marbling a Scarf

1. Referring to "Marbling Trays" on pages 87–89, build a temporary tray that is 4" longer and wider than your scarf. For example, if your scarf is 8" x 54", build a 12" x 58" tray.

2. Cover your worktable with a plastic drop cloth. Gather your tools and materials.

3. Fill the tray with marbling base.

4. Follow the directions for "Marbling" on pages 25–28. Marble the scarf with the hem side up.

5. Allow fabric to dry. Heat-set, following the paint manufacturer's instructions.

6. Iron a temporary stabilizer under the area where you will sign your name. Using a gold or silver Pilot pen, sign your work!

Hint

To sign your work, press an iron-on stabilizer such as Sulky's Totally Stable onto the wrong side of your fabric (the side you won't be signing). Using a Pilot or Pigma pen, sign your name on the stiffened fabric. Tear away the stabilizer.

Treasure bags

Treasure Bag

TREASURE BAGS ARE perfect for gifts. Make small bags to hold a sachet or thimble for a quilting friend, large bags for bottles of wine.

You may want to experiment with the variations on page 61. Be creative! Think of fun ways to embellish your bags, for example:

♦ Use pinking or scalloping shears to trim the top edge.
♦ Unravel the top edge.
♦ Turn the top edge down as a cuff, so you see how the fabric appeared before it was marbled.
♦ Tie a bag with raffia or other interesting material.

These instructions are for the bag shown in the bottom right of the photo.

You Will Need

♦ 1½ yds. of decorative cording (½" diameter or smaller)
♦ 16" x 20" piece of marbled fabric (for a 9½" x 14½" bag)
♦ Iron and ironing board
♦ Rotary cutter, cutting guide, and self-healing mat (optional)
♦ Sewing supplies
♦ Tape
♦ Thread

Making a Treasure Bag

1. To make a casing for the decorative cord, fold a 20"-long side of the marbled fabric under ¼", then ¾". Beginning 1½" from one end, stitch along the bottom. Stop stitching 1½" from the other end.

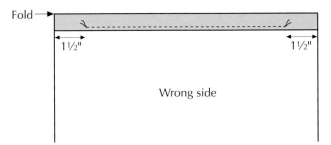

2. Fold the fabric in half widthwise, right sides together.

3. Using a ½"-wide seam allowance, stitch down the side and across the bottom of the bag. Backstitch at the beginning and end.

4. Turn the bag right side out. Press.

5. Tape one end of the cording, then gently push it through the casing. Knot the cording ends to the desired length, then trim.

Painted Leaves Pillow

FOR THIS PILLOW, you will use the resist and techniques on page 54. Although I've provided templates for the leaves, you may want to design shapes more suitable to your home. Make a lovely Christmas gift by embellishing a pillow with holiday shapes.

Finished Size: 12" x 14"

You Will Need

♦ ¾ yd. of 44"-wide fabric, pretreated in alum bath (see page 18)
♦ Adhesive material, such as PeelnStick (see page 15)
♦ Embroidery hoop
♦ Iron and ironing board
♦ Marbling materials and tools (see page 25)
♦ Paintbrush
♦ Pencil
♦ Pigma pen for leaf veins
♦ Pillow form, 12" x 14" (see page 71)
♦ Rotary cutter, cutting guide, and self-healing mat (optional)
♦ Scissors
♦ Sewing machine and supplies
♦ Silk paints in your preferred colors
♦ Silk resist, such as Deka silk resist or PRO Chemical & Dye's Sabra silk resist
♦ Template material

Painted Leaves Pillow

Marbling the Fabric

1. Make templates from the leaf patterns on page 71. Using the templates, trace leaves from the adhesive material (or create your own shapes).

2. Cut the pretreated fabric into 2 pieces, each 20" x 24". Measure and lightly mark the center of 1 fabric rectangle. Set the other piece aside.

3. Remove the paper backing from the leaf shapes. Arrange the leaves in the center on the right side of the marked fabric rectangle. Press in place.

4. Marble both fabric rectangles, following the steps on pages 25–28. The shapes usually fall off in the rinse; if they don't, remove them after rinsing.

5. Place the leaf fabric in an embroidery hoop, centering the shapes.

6. Apply silk resist to the edge where the marbling meets the resist shape as shown on page 54. Allow the silk resist to dry (about 1 hour).

7. Using a paintbrush, apply silk paint inside the resist lines, working from the center toward the edges of the shape.

8. Allow paint to dry. Heat-set, following the paint manufacturer's instructions.

9. To remove the resist, soak the fabric in water.

10. To add the leaf veins, use a Pigma pen. Stabilize the fabric as described on page 67 before drawing. Heat-set the pen markings.

Making the Pillow

Use a ½"-wide seam allowance.

1. For the pillow front, cut the leaf fabric into a 13" x 15" rectangle, centering the leaves. Make sure the leaves are centered before cutting out the rectangle.

2. For the pillow back, cut the second rectangle into 2 pieces, each 10" x 13". Fold over a long edge of each 10" x 13" rectangle ¼", then ¾". Stitch.

Pillow front   Pillow backs

3. Lay the pillow front on your sewing table, right side up. Place a hemmed rectangle on the front, then place the other rectangle on top (hemmed edges will overlap). Match the edges. Pin.

4. Stitch around the pillow, using a ½"-wide seam allowance. Remove pins. (For sharper corners, trim the corners.)

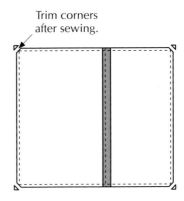

Trim corners
after sewing.

5. Turn right side out and press. Insert the pillow form.

PILLOW FORM

Finished Size: 12" x 14"

You Will Need

- ♦ ½ yd. of 44"-wide muslin
- ♦ Fiberfill pillow stuffing
- ♦ Iron and ironing board
- ♦ Rotary cutter, cutting guide, and self-healing mat (optional)
- ♦ Sewing machine and supplies

Making a Pillow Form

Use a ½"-wide seam allowance.

1. From the muslin, cut 2 rectangles, each 13½" x 15½".

2. Pin the 2 rectangles, right sides together. Stitch around the rectangles, using a ½"-wide seam allowance. Leave a 3"-wide opening for stuffing.

3. Turn right side out. Stuff with fiberfill.

4. Hand or machine stitch the opening closed.

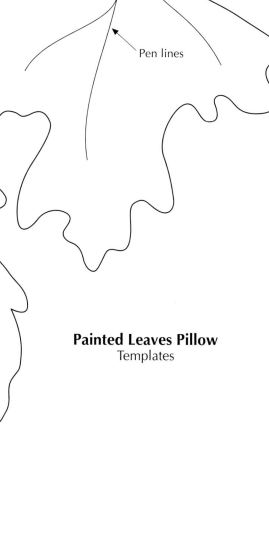

Pen lines

Pen lines

Painted Leaves Pillow
Templates

Soup-can prints

Soup-Can Prints

MAKING PRINTS ON fabric squares with a soup can is a unique way to make quilt blocks. You can use the squares as is or as the centers of larger blocks. You use a small (8" x 8") pan or a clean butter tub as a marbling tray, small pieces of fabric, and very little paint.

Finished Block Size: 8" x 8"

You Will Need

- ¾ yd. of fabric, pretreated in alum bath (see page 18).
- Marbling materials and tools (see page 25)
- Masking tape
- Pencil
- Plastic drop cloth
- Rotary cutter, cutting guide, and self-healing mat (optional)
- Rubber bands
- Scissors
- Small pan, 8" x 8", clean butter tub, or disposable aluminum pie pan
- Soup can (2½" to 3" diameter)

Marbling the Blocks

Refer to the directions for "Marbling" on pages 25–28.

1. Cover your worktable with a plastic drop cloth. Gather your tools and materials.

2. From the pretreated fabric, cut 9" squares. A ¾-yd piece of fabric will make 15 blocks. (Cut squares approximately 1" larger than your desired finished block.)

3. Finger-press 1 fabric square in half, then in half again to find the center. Center the fabric, right side up, on the bottom of the can. Secure with a rubber band.

4. Wrap the bottom edge of the can with masking tape. (This step prevents your marbling colors from migrating up the can sides.)

5. Drop the marbling colors onto the base. Using a stylus, gently swirl the colors as shown.

6. Lower the bottom of the can until it touches the swirled paints. Hold in place for a few seconds. Hold the can perpendicular to the marbling base.

7. Lift the can straight up. Do not turn the can from side to side; paint will drip on the rest of the fabric.

8. Rinse, holding the can perpendicular to the water as shown.

Hint

Use a variety of fabrics and can sizes for interesting blocks.

9. Rinse the fabric square, remove the rubber band and tape, then rinse again. (The tape helps keep paint from migrating.)

10. Repeat steps 3–9 for each of the remaining fabric squares.

11. Allow fabric to dry. Heat-set, following the paint manufacturer's instructions.

Step 5 of Marbling the Blocks

Step 6 of Marbling the Blocks

Step 8 of Marbling the Blocks

Fancy Scallops vest

Fancy Scallops Vest

FOR THIS PARTICULAR vest, I used the Nonpareil pattern (see page 00) on a mottled gold fabric. Because I wanted the background fabric to show, I used color-less extender as well as complementary marbling colors.

When you choose fabric for scalloping, look for colors that complement the marbled fabric. If you need help, choose one dark color and use it in a narrow strip as an accent, then choose one medium color for a wider strip. In this vest, I chose to use a color that almost matches the background fabric for the wider strip.

Before you begin, read the suggestions for choosing a pattern on page 55.

You Will Need

- 1 yd. of paper-backed fusible web
- ¼ yd. each of 2 different solid fabrics for scallops
- Colorless extender
- Commercial vest pattern with a straight hemline
- Decorative threads to match fabrics
- Embroidery hoop with a spring closure
- Fabric for vest lining (Refer to pattern instructions for yardage.)
- Fabric for vest, pretreated in alum bath (see page 18) (Refer to pattern instructions for yardage; add ½ yd. for "insurance.")
- Iron and ironing board
- Marbling materials and tools (see page 25)
- Pencil
- Plastic drop cloth
- Scissors
- Sewing machine and supplies
- Teflon pressing cloth to protect ironing board (optional)
- Transparent nylon thread
- Water-soluble stabilizer

Marbling the Fabric

1. Cover your worktable with a plastic drop cloth. Gather your tools and materials. Choose a marbling tray large enough for the largest pattern piece. You can also use a larger tray to marble several pattern pieces at once.

2. Refer to "Figuring Marbled Fabric for Garments" on page 79. Marble the pre-treated vest fabric, following the steps on pages 25–28. Rinse, dry, and heat-set the fabric.

Making the Vest

1. Cut out the vest pieces. Make sure pattern scallops are pointing down.

2. From the fusible web, cut 3 strips, each 2" by the width of a vest front or back. From the lining fabric and coordinating solid fabrics, cut 1 strip, each 2" by the width of a vest front or back.

3. Following the manufacturer's instructions, iron a fusible-web strip to the wrong side of a vest front. Do not remove the paper backing.

4. Using your scissors, trim curves on the hemline of the vest front. Follow the curves of your marbled pattern. Remove the paper backing from the fusible web.

5. Iron a strip of fusible web to the wrong side of each solid fabric strip.

6. Position the first solid fabric strip, right side up, along the vest bottom, extending about 1" beyond the scalloped edge. Iron.

7. Trim the fabric strip ¼" to ½", loosely matching the scalloped edge. Remove the paper backing from the fusible web.

8. Remove the paper backing from the back of the second solid color. Iron a lining strip to the colored fabric strip.

9. Position the second solid fabric strip, right side up, along the vest bottom, again extending about 1" beyond the scalloped edge. Iron, then trim to match previous scallops.

10. To finish the scallop edges, thread your sewing machine with transparent nylon thread in the bobbin and decorative thread on the top. Using a free-motion or satin stitch, machine appliqué the scalloped edges.

    For the last scalloped edge, place the edge of the fabric on top of water-soluble stabilizer. Place in an embroidery hoop with a spring closure.

11. Repeat steps 2–10 for the remaining vest pieces.

Assembling the Vest

Make the vest, following the pattern instructions. Fold the edge of the lining inside ¼", then ¾". Press. Tack the lining hem above the scalloped edge.

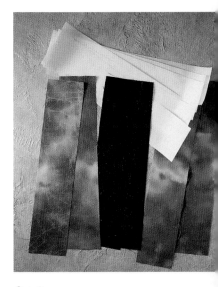

Step 2

Step 4

Steps 9 and 10

He Loves Me vest

He Loves Me Vest

I LOVE THE country charm of homespun. When used as a background fabric for marbling, it takes on a sophistication all its own. Even though there is a slight texture to the fabric, it marbles beautifully. I use a lot of colorless extender and no more than two marbling colors so the background fabric is not obscured by the marbling.

For this particular vest, I used a blue-black paint, a bright yellow paint, and colorless extender to marble the Waved Icarus pattern. I further emphasized the colors by repeating them in the appliqués along the bottom of the vest.

I love "lining art." The daisy missing one petal recalls the beginning of a favorite childhood pastime—plucking petals off a flower to see if he does indeed love me!

You Will Need

- ♦ 1 yd. of paper-backed fusible web
- ♦ Assorted fabric scraps for daisies and leaves
- ♦ Commercial vest pattern with a straight hemline
- ♦ Decorative threads to match fabrics
- ♦ Embroidery hoop with a spring closure
- ♦ Fabric for vest lining (Refer to pattern instructions for yardage.)
- ♦ Fabric for vest, pretreated in alum bath (see page 18) (Refer to pattern instructions for yardage; add ½ yd. for "insurance.")
- ♦ Iron and ironing board
- ♦ Marbling materials and tools (see page 25)
- ♦ Pencil and scissors
- ♦ Sewing machine and supplies
- ♦ Teflon pressing cloth to protect ironing board (optional)
- ♦ Template material
- ♦ Transparent nylon thread
- ♦ Water-soluble stabilizer
- ♦ Totally Stable tear-away stabilizer

Hint

Consider embellishing your marbled pieces with antique buttons. I use these on every garment I create, but I'm passionate about the kinship between antique buttons and marbled fabric. Both have a history.

I pieced the vest below from a marbled homespun, then embellished it with three different antique black-glass buttons. Using a variety of buttons creates interest. (I never use matched sets of buttons, even if I have them.)

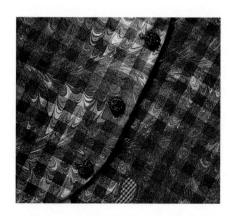

Marbling the Fabric

1. Cover your worktable with a plastic drop cloth. Gather your tools and materials. Choose a marbling tray large enough for the largest pattern piece. You can also use a larger tray to marble several pattern pieces at once.

2. Refer to "Figuring Marbled Fabric for Garments" on page 79. Marble the pre-treated fabric, following the steps on pages 25–28. Rinse, dry, and heat-set the fabric.

Appliquéing the Vest Fronts

1. Cut out the vest pieces, leaving approximately 3" extra at the front bottom edges.

2. Mark the cutting line on the bottom of a vest front. This becomes your placement line for appliqués.

3. Following the manufacturer's instructions, iron fusible web to the wrong sides of the assorted daisy and leaf fabrics. Do not remove the paper backing.

4. Prepare templates for the daisies and leaves on page 78.

5. Using the templates, cut out the daisy pieces and leaves from the assorted fabrics.

6. Remove the paper backing, then arrange the appliqué pieces on a vest front. (Follow the placement line.) Iron in place. Repeat for the other vest front.

7. Iron tear-away stabilizer underneath the appliqués.

8. To finish the daisy and leaf edges, thread your sewing machine with transparent nylon thread in the bobbin and decorative thread on the top. Using a free-motion or satin stitch, machine appliqué the top edge to the placement line. Remove the stabilizer.

9. Cut away excess fabric from the bottom edge. Back the appliqués with a water-soluble stabilizer. Place the area in an embroidery hoop. Machine appliqué the bottom edge.

10. Repeat steps 8–9 for the other vest front.

Step 9

Assembling the Vest

Make the vest, following the pattern instructions. Attach the lining at the armholes, neckline edges, and down the front. Allow the lining to hang freely at the bottom.

For vests with irregular hemlines (created by appliqués or other forms of machine art), it can be difficult to attach the lining. Since the lining was cut out following the original pattern, the hemline should be clearly marked.

Fold the edge of the lining inside ¼", then ¾". Press. Stitch along the edge, using a straight stitch. If desired, you can tack the lining hem to the inside of the vest bottom at the side seams.

Daisy
Cut 1 and 1 reversed

He Loves Me Vest
Templates

Petal
Cut 2 and 2 reversed

Daisy
Cut 1 and 1 reversed;
cut 1 for lining and
remove 1 petal

Petal
Cut 1

Figuring Marbled Fabric for Garments

In preparing fabric for a garment, it's hard to know how many pieces to marble—especially if the garment has many pattern pieces like the jacket on page 62. Use the following system for figuring the amount of fabric to marble.

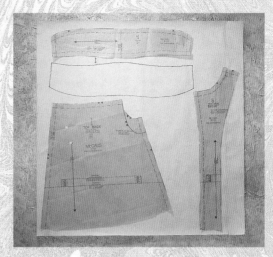

Pattern pieces laid out in a "paper tray"

1. Lay out the pattern pieces. Be sure to read the instructions carefully; many pattern pieces will need doubles or a place on the fold.

2. Choose a marbling tray large enough to accommodate the largest pattern piece. (You may be able to marble several pieces at once in a larger tray.)

3. Cut a piece of paper the size of the tray, or use masking tape to mask an area the same size as your tray.

4. Lay as many of the pieces as possible within the paper tray. (Be sure the pieces all face the right direction, and don't forget about fold lines.) One tray-size piece of paper represents one piece of fabric. Repeat this process until you have determined how much fabric you need to cut out all the pattern pieces. *As you work, make a list of the pieces you laid out for each piece of fabric. Refer to this list when you trace and cut your pattern pieces.*

♦ Allow several inches between the edges of your marbling tray and the fabric pieces.

♦ When you're tackling a large project, marble all the fabric in the same session. It's hard to re-create (or remember) the amounts of color and the patterning rhythm.

♦ Try to lay 2 fronts or 2 backs on the same fabric piece. Pieces next to each other in a garment have more continuity if cut from the same piece of fabric.

♦ Lay the pattern on paper as if it were on fabric; follow the grain line. This can make a difference in the amount of fabric to marble.

♦ Most marbling patterns are one-way designs; lay all pieces in the same direction.

♦ Allow several inches between each pattern piece; fabric draws up when each piece is quilted.

♦ Remember, most pattern pieces require a double (for example, "cut 1 and 1 reversed") as well as a "place on fold." Be sure to allow enough fabric. For peace of mind, marble extra fabric.

Falling Leaves quilt

Falling Leaves Quilt

THIS QUILT PATTERN is based on a "No Templates Required" class taught by Barbara Butler. The block, Indian Hatchet, is an old one, but the innovative way Barbara manipulates the blocks and creates the borders makes an exciting quilt.

For more information on the techniques used in this pattern, see "Using Resists" on pages 50–54 and "Stamping" on page 55.

Finished Size: 26½" x 37½"

You Will Need

- ½ yd. of batik fabric for borders
- ½ yd. of medium print fabric, pretreated in alum bath (see page 18)
- ¾ yd. of dark solid fabric (Pretreat ½ yd. in alum bath.)
- ¾ yd. of light fabric for block centers, pretreated in alum bath
- ¼ yd. of light fabric for pleated inner border
- Adhesive shelf paper
- Couching thread, such as Candlelight or Glamour (optional)
- Decorative threads to match fabrics
- Iron and ironing board
- Lumiére metallic textile paint
- Marbling materials and tools (see page 25)
- Pencil
- Plastic plate, 1 for each color of paint
- Plastic spoon, 1 for each color of paint
- Rotary cutter, cutting guide, and self-healing mat
- Scissors
- Sewing machine and supplies
- Stamps, no more than 3" wide (see page 16)
- Transparent nylon thread
- 1 yd. of 100% cotton, low-loft batting
- 1 yd. of fabric for backing
- ½ yd. of fabric for binding

Marbling the Fabric

1. Cover your worktable with a plastic drop cloth. Gather your tools and materials.

2. Marble the ½ yd. medium print fabric, following the steps on pages 25–28. Rinse, dry, and heat-set the fabric.

Cutting the Block Pieces

Use your rotary cutter, cutting guide, and self-healing mat.

1. From the light fabric, cut 12 squares, each 6" x 6".

2. From the ½ yard of pretreated dark solid, cut 12 squares, each 6" x 6".

3. From the remaining ¼ yard of dark solid, cut 24 squares, each 4" x 4".

4. From the marbled print, cut 24 squares, each 4" x 4".

Applying the Self-Adhesive Resist

1. Fold each of the 12 dark 6" squares in half on the diagonal. Lightly press.

2. Draw or trace a shape on a piece of adhesive shelf paper. Cut 12 shapes from the shelf paper.

3. Remove the paper backing, then press a shape in the center of each fabric square as shown.

4. Marble each square, following the steps on pages 25–28. Remove the adhesive. Rinse, dry, and heat-set the fabric.

Steps 3 and 4 of Applying the Self-Adhesive Resist

Making the Blocks

Use a ¼"-wide seam allowance.

1. On the wrong side of each 4" square, draw a diagonal line from corner to corner.

2. On each light 6" square, lay 2 marbled 4" squares as shown, right sides together. Pin. Stitch along the marked line on the 4" squares.

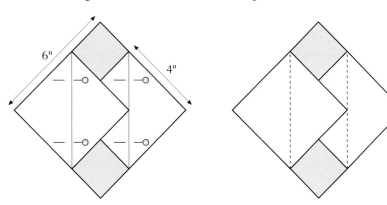

Step 3 of Making the Blocks

Step 4 of Making the Blocks

3. Using your rotary-cutting supplies, trim the excess corner fabrics ¼" from the seam.

4. Repeat steps 2–4 for the dark 6" and 4" squares. Be sure to center the resist shapes between the 4" blocks. Press all blocks.

   If desired, embellish the seams with couching thread. Use a transparent nylon thread on top of your sewing machine, and regular thread in the bobbin. Lay couching thread on top of the seam lines if desired. Using a narrow zigzag stitch, sew the couching thread in place.

Assembling and Finishing the Quilt

Use a ¼"-wide seam allowance.

1. Referring to the photo on page 64, arrange the quilt blocks.

2. Join the rows, alternating the seam allowances between the blocks and rows.

3. Stamp the quilt top, following the steps on page 55. Allow the paint to dry.

4. From the remaining ¼ yard of light fabric, cut 2 strips, each 1" x 33½", and 2 strips, each 1" x 22", for the pleated inner borders. Fold the strips in half lengthwise; press. Place the side borders on the quilt top, right sides together and raw edges matching. Stitch. Repeat for the top and bottom borders.

5. From the ½ yard of dark batik fabric, cut 2 strips, each 2½" x 42", and 2 strips, each 2½" x 27", for the outer borders.

6. Measure each edge of the quilt top and mark the center of each side with a pin. Fold each border in half and mark the center with a pin.

7. Pin the top border to the quilt top, matching the centers. Stitch, beginning and ending ¼" from each edge of the quilt top. Repeat for the remaining borders.

8. Lay the first corner to be mitered on the ironing board. Fold under one border strip at a 45° angle to the other strip. Press and pin.

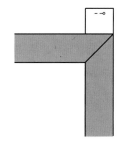

9. Fold the quilt with right sides together, lining up the edges of the border. Stitch on the crease, sewing from the inside corner to the outside edge. Press the seam open and trim excess border fabric, leaving a ¼" seam allowance.

Pressed crease

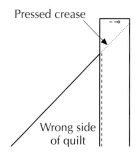

Wrong side of quilt

10. Repeat steps 8 and 9 for the remaining corners.

11. Layer the quilt top, batting, and backing. Baste.

12. Quilt as desired or follow the suggestions on pages 90–91. Trim excess batting and backing even with the quilt top.

13. To determine the length of the binding, measure the perimeter of the quilt and add 10".

14. From the ½ yard of binding fabric, cut 1¼"-wide strips on the straight of grain to equal the total measurement in step 13. Seam strips as necessary. Fold the seamed binding strip in half lengthwise, wrong sides together, and press.

15. Stitch binding to the quilt sides, trimming at the top and bottom. Fold the binding to the back and hand stitch. Stitch binding to the top and bottom of the quilt, trimming approximately ½" beyond the quilt. Fold the cut ends over ½", then fold the binding back and hand stitch.

Don't forget to sign your quilt.

Hint

If you aren't sure where to stamp, make several paper stamps and move them around on your quilt top until you like the look.

Appendixes

Marbling Rakes and Combs

MARBLING RAKES AND combs are easy to make. You can use materials you have on hand, such as drapery hooks, wig T-pins, or curler pins, for the rake tines. Wooden rakes and combs are a bit more work, but are much more durable than those made from foam core or cardboard.

The process for making rakes and combs is the same; the difference is the distance between the tines. Attach rake tines at 1" intervals. Attach comb tines at ⅜" to ⅝" intervals.

You may want to experiment with different types of rakes and combs. Varying the space between tines creates different effects.

Always store rakes and combs so the tines won't bend out of shape. I store mine on a pegboard with 10"-long brackets. I screw a cup hook on the end of each rake, then hook it over the bracket. This allows me to store a lot of rakes (more than one hundred) in a small space.

WOOD RAKE OR COMB

MANY PATTERNS REQUIRE raking across the width as well as the length of the marbling tray. Ideally, you should have two rakes, one for the width of the tray and one for the length. To get started, I recommend making a rake or comb a little longer than the outside measurement of the marbling tray. When you rake the width of the tray, you can straddle the sides of the tray or remove unnecessary tines. I feel that I get better control and leverage by resting a rake on the edges of the tray as I work, but you may prefer to make a shorter rake.

You Will Need
- ¼"-thick wood (balsa and pine work well)
- Drill and bits
- Paintbrush
- Pencil and ruler
- Plastic curler pins, wig T-pins (available at beauty-supply shops), or long quilter's pins (at least 1½" long)*
- Polyurethane paint
- Saw

*The finer the tine point, the less drag on the paint, and the finer the print.

Hint

For a quick and easy rake, use a yardstick as a base. Use the measurement lines instead of measuring and marking. Or, use drapery hooks and hang them over a piece of wood at marked intervals.

Making the Rake

1. Cut the wood into strips that are ½" wide and the length of your marbling tray plus 2". For example, if the outside measurements of the tray are 22" x 28", cut the wood into ½" x 30" strips.

2. Using your pencil and ruler, draw a line down the center of the wood. Measuring from one end, make marks at 1" intervals along the line. (For a comb, make marks at ⅜" to ⅝" intervals.)

3. Drill holes (based on the diameter of the tines) through the 1" marks.

4. Using the paintbrush, apply 2 or 3 coats of polyurethane paint. Refer to the manufacturer's label for application instructions, safety precautions, and drying times. Dry thoroughly between coats.

5. Insert the pins through the holes. Be sure they fit snugly.

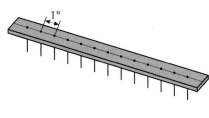

FOAM CORE OR CARDBOARD RAKE OR COMB

You Will Need

- ¼"-thick foam core or heavy cardboard
- Duct tape, electrical tape, or polyurethane paint and paintbrush
- Pencil and ruler
- Plastic curler pins, wig T-pins (available at beauty-supply shops), or long quilter's pins (at least 1½" long)
- Scissors, or X-Acto knife and ruler
- Waterproof glue

Making the Rake

1. Using the scissors, or X-Acto knife and ruler, cut 2 strips of foam core or cardboard, each ¾" wide by the inside length of the tray. (The tines are usually shorter than those on a wood rake because of the core; make this type of rake so it fits inside the tray.)

2. Measuring from one end of a strip, make marks at 1" intervals. (For a comb, make marks at ⅜" to ⅝" intervals.)

3. Place a drop of glue on each mark made in step 2, then press the pins into the glue. Allow to dry, referring to the glue manufacturer's instructions.

4. Place a line of glue around the edges of the second strip, then press the strips together and allow to dry.

5. Cover the rake or comb with duct tape or electrical tape, or seal with polyurethane paint as described for the wood rake or comb. Allow paint to dry for at least 24 hours before using.

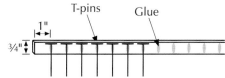

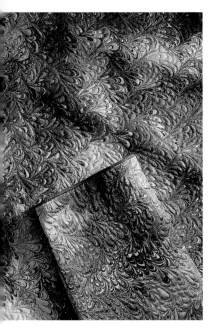

Bouquet pattern

BOUQUET COMB

A BOUQUET COMB has two alternating rows of tines. It's only used for a few patterns, but the patterns are so exquisite, making a bouquet comb is well worth the effort.

I have many combs that don't fall into the traditional definition of bouquet combs. Some have different spacing between the rows of tines; some have different spacing between the tines along the same row. The effect of the different spacing is marvelous. Don't hesitate to experiment.

You Will Need

- ♦ ¼"-thick wood (balsa and pine work well)
- ♦ Drill and bits
- ♦ Paintbrush
- ♦ Pencil and ruler
- ♦ Plastic curler pins, wig T-pins (available at beauty-supply shops), or long quilter's pins (at least 1½" long)
- ♦ Polyurethane paint
- ♦ Saw

Making the Comb

1. Cut the wood into strips that are 2" wide and the length of your marbling tray plus 2". For example, if the outside measurements of your tray are 22" x 28", cut the wood into 2" x 30" strips.

2. Using a pencil and ruler, draw 2 lines ½" in along each long edge.

3. Measuring from one end, make marks at 2" intervals along one line. Measuring along the second line, make marks every 2", alternating them halfway between the first set of marks.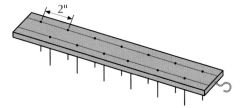

4. Drill holes (based on the diameter of the tines) through the pencil marks.

5. Using a paintbrush, apply 2 or 3 coats of polyurethane paint. Refer to the manufacturer's label for application instructions, safety precautions, and drying times. Dry thoroughly between coats.

6. Insert the pins through the holes. Be sure they fit snugly.

Broom-Corn Whisk

You Will Need

- Broom corn
- Rubber bands and/or twine (I use both. Rubber bands provide a tight grip, but the material disintegrates. Twine doesn't grip as well, but it lasts longer.)
- Scissors

Broom-corn whisk

Making the Whisk

1. Cut 6" lengths of broom corn until you have a 1"-diameter bundle.

2. Using the rubber bands and/or twine, bind the bundle of broom corn twice. Bind approximately 1" to 1½" from one end with a rubber band, then wrap twine on top of the rubber band for extra strength and durability.

    To clean your whisks, soak them in warm water, then use a rag or brush to scrub the bristles clean. Spread the bristles apart to dry.

Marbling Trays

TO DETERMINE THE size of tray you'll use most frequently, ask yourself the following questions: "What kind of quilts and garments do I make? What size fabric will best suit my needs?" My favorite tray size is 22" x 28". This size works well for many items, including vests, small clothing pieces, and fat quarters. I use a 30" x 40" tray for larger pieces.

If you make garments, look at your pattern pieces. The tray should be a little bigger than the largest piece. Look at the bodice of "Tiger Lily Princess" at right. Because my largest pattern piece was 8" x 20", I was able to use a fairly small tray to accomplish this wonderful effect.

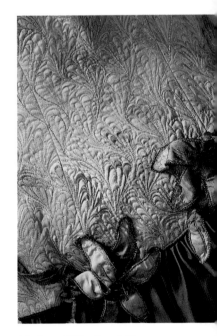

The beautiful bodice of this gown was marbled in a small tray.

TEMPORARY MARBLING TRAY

THE BIG ADVANTAGE of this tray is that you don't have to paint it, and you can easily take it apart for storage. Temporary trays are good for odd-size items that you don't marble often, such as long, narrow silk scarves.

You Will Need

- 4-mil plastic sheeting (available at building-supply stores)
- 4 pieces of wood (pine works well), each 1" x 4" x your desired length (For example, if your desired tray size is 22" x 28", you will need two 22"-long pieces and two 30"-long pieces.)
- Hammer and nails
- Scissors
- Staple gun

Temporary marbling tray

Making the Tray

1. Fit the 4 wood pieces together to make a frame; use nails to secure.

2. From the plastic sheeting, cut a square or rectangle that is large enough to completely line the inside and outside edges of your frame. If you're using 1" x 4" wood pieces, add approximately 18" to the width and length of your plastic sheeting. For example, if your frame is a 22" x 28" rectangle, cut a 40" x 46" rectangle from the plastic sheeting.

3. Place the frame on your worktable. Line the frame with the plastic-sheeting rectangle you cut. The plastic should touch the surface on the inside of the frame; this creates a bottom.

4. Using a staple gun, staple the plastic sheeting to the outside frame edges as shown.

PERMANENT MARBLING TRAY

You Will Need

- 4 pieces of wood, each 1" x 4" x your desired length (For example, if your desired tray size is 22" x 28", you will need two 22"-long pieces and two 30"-long pieces.)
- 1 piece of ½"-thick plywood, cut to fit the bottom of your desired frame size (For example, cut plywood 24" x 30" for a 22" x 28" tray. Or use a saw to trim plywood flush to the frame after assembly.)
- Drill and a bit to match the plug size if desired
- Hammer and finishing nails
- Paintbrush
- Rubber plug (This is optional. It's easier and less messy to drain your marbling base through a hole in the bottom of the tray than by pouring it over the edge.)
- Sandpaper, fine
- Scissors
- Waterproof caulking
- White polyurethane or enamel paint
- Wood glue

Making the Tray

1. Fit the 4 wood pieces together to make a frame; use nails to secure.

2. Spread a line of wood glue along the bottom edge of the frame. Lay the piece of plywood on top of the glued edges, matching corners.

3. Nail the plywood bottom to the frame, placing a finishing nail every 3".

4. If desired, drill a hole in the plywood bottom, matching the plug diameter. The plug should be a tight fit.

5. Using fine sandpaper, lightly sand the tray to prevent splinters. Remove wood dust.

6. Use waterproof caulking to seal all joints. Allow to dry and cure, following the manufacturer's instructions.

7. Using a paintbrush, apply 2 or 3 coats of white polyurethane or enamel paint. Refer to the manufacturer's label for application instructions, safety precautions, and drying times. Dry thoroughly between coats.

I have many marbling trays, but not as many as I would like. To increase the versatility of my trays, I use a wooden wedge to adjust the inner dimensions.

To make a wedge, cut a 1" x 4" board to the inside width of your tray. Be sure the wedge fits *snugly* across the inside of the tray. I use a hammer to fit the wedge in place. A snug fit prevents the marbling base from leaking to the other side of the tray. (The base will eventually leak through the wedge, but this works well for a short marbling session.)

If the tray is already filled with base and I want to marble a small piece of fabric, I use a wedge to prevent paint from spreading farther than needed, giving me more control.

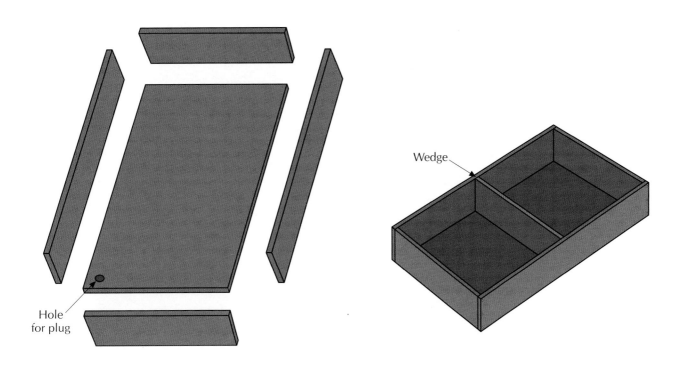

Hole for plug

Wedge

Quilting Marbled Fabric

QUILTING ADDS INCREDIBLE depth and movement to marbled fabric. I love to use quilted marbled fabric in garments. The garments lose some drapability, but the stitching adds so much dimension that it's worth it.

Decorative threads such as rayon, metallic, Mylar, variegated, and silk all work well.

For batting, I recommend a low-loft, 100% cotton batting, such as Soft Touch by Fairfield.

Quilting marbled fabric really brings out the pattern.

QUILTING

THESE INSTRUCTIONS ARE for a garment.

1. Lay the pattern pieces on your marbled fabric, referring to your list of pattern pieces. Trace. Mark approximately 1" beyond the cutting line.

2. Layer backing fabric, batting, and marbled fabric. Pin-baste.

   For garments, use an ultra-lightweight material, such as tulle or pattern duplicating material, for the backing fabric.

3. Thread your sewing machine with transparent nylon thread in the bobbin and decorative thread on the top.

4. Place the layered piece in an embroidery hoop with a spring closure. (This type of hoop can be released and moved to different parts of the fabric while still under the presser foot.)

5. Using a free-motion stitch, machine quilt the marbled design. Stitch to the edge of the marked lines. This type of machine work is tedious; I mark around the pieces and just quilt to the lines.

6. Lay pattern pieces within the boundaries of the marked lines. Pin. Cut out the marbled pattern pieces.

   Some of my garments have as many as twenty pieces. (For an example, look at the jacket on page 62). I don't recommend this for your first project. Start with a simple vest like the one on page 76. For more information on machine quilting, see "Further Reading" on page 93.

Quilting adds depth and dimension.

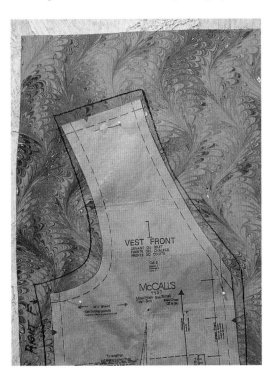

Step 1

Step 2

Resources

DHARMA TRADING COMPANY

PO Box 150916
San Rafael, CA 94915
1-800-542-5227 or fax 415-456-8747
E-mail: catalog@dharmatrading.com
Web site: www.dharmatrading.com
Textile paints, marbling supplies, silk paints and resists; free catalog

EARTH GUILD

33 Haywood Street
Asheville, NC 28801
1-800-327-8448 or fax 828-255-8593
E-mail: inform@earthguild.com
Web site: www.earthguild.com
Miscellaneous craft materials; free introductory catalog

G & S DYE

250 Dundas Street West, Unit #8
Toronto, Ontario M5T 2Z5
Canada
1-800-596-0550 or fax 416-596-0493
E-mail: gsdye@interlog.com
Web site: www.interlog.com/~gsdye
Textile paints, marbling supplies, silk paints and resists, silk fabric and scarves; free catalog

HANCOCKS OF PADUCAH

3841 Hinkleville Road
Paducah, Kentucky 42001
1-800-845-8723
E-mail: Hanpad@sunsix.infi.net
Web site: www.Hancocks-Paducah.com
Soft Touch batting and other quilting supplies; free catalog

PRO CHEMICAL & DYE, INC.

PO Box 14
Somerset, MA 02726
1-508-676-3838 (information)
1-800-2-BUY-DYE (ordering)
E-mail: PRO-CHEMICAL@worldnet.att.net
Web site: www.prochemical.com
Marbling supplies, silk-paint resist; free catalog

TALAS

568 Broadway
New York, New York 10012
212-736-7744 or fax 212-219-0735
E-mail: talas@sprynet.com
Marbling supplies, rakes, combs, trays; catalog: $6.00

THAI SILKS

252F State Street
Los Altos, CA 94022
1-800-722-SILK or fax 1-415-948-3426
E-mail: thaisilk@pacbell.net
Web site: www.thaisilk.com
Silk fabrics and silk-scarf "blanks"; free price list

Further Reading

Barnes, Christine. *Color: The Quilter's Guide.* Bothell, Wash.: That Patchwork Place, 1997.

Dietrich, Mimi. *Borders and Bindings.* Bothell, Wash: That Patchwork Place, 1998.

Doak, Carol. *Your First Quilt Book (or is should be!).* Bothell, Wash: That Patchwork Place, 1998.

Dunnewold, Jane. *Complex Cloth.* Bothell, Wash.: Fiber Studio Press, 1996.

Lauer, David A. *Design Basics,* 3rd ed. New York: Holt, Reinhart and Winston, 1990.

Noble, Elin. *Dyes & Paints.* Bothell, Wash.: Fiber Studio Press, 1998.

Noble, Maurine. Machine *Quilting Made Easy.* Bothell, Wash.: That Patchwork Place, 1994.

Penders, Mary Coyne. *Color and Cloth: The Quilmaker's Ultimate Workbook.* San Francisco: Quilt Digest Press, 1989.

Simmons, Judy. *Machine Needlelace and Other Embellishment Techniques.* Bothell, Wash.: That Patchwork Place, 1997.

Wolfrom, Joen. *The Magical Effects of Color.* Martinez, Calif.: C&T Publishing, 1992.

Bibliography

Dunnewold, Jane. *Complex Cloth.* Bothell, Wash.: That Patchwork Place, 1996.

Maurer, Diane Vogel and Paul. *Marbling.* New York: Crescent Books, 1991.

Taylor, Carol et al. *Marbling Paper & Fabric.* New York: Sterling Publishing Co., 1991.

Wolfe, Richard J. *Marbled Paper: Its History, Techniques and Patterns.* Philadelphia: University of Pennsylvania Press, 1990.

Index

Meet the Artist

Judy Simmons grew up in New York, surrounded by talented and high-spirited women who believed nothing was impossible. She has always had a passion for fiber and began sewing doll clothes at a very young age. Judy majored in home economics and earned a teaching degree from Oneonta State University in New York. She taught for many years before venturing out on her own.

Her love of fiber and fiber-related art forms initiated her interest in surface-design techniques. She is self-taught in all areas of surface design. She loves to make creative clothing as well as art quilts, using various forms of surface design along with creative machine techniques.

Judy's award-winning quilts and wearables have been exhibited throughout the country and internationally. She is a six-time designer for the prestigious Fairfield Fashion Show. In addition, her work has been published in *Quilter's Newsletter Magazine, Quilt, American Quilter, Sewing and Fine Needlework, McCall's Quilting, Craft and Needlework Age, Lady's Circle Patchwork Quilts, Quilt World,* and *Patchwork Quilt Tsushin,* as well as numerous books and calendars.

Judy has taught and lectured throughout the United States as well as in Canada and Japan.

Selected Titles from Fiber Studio Press and That Patchwork Place

Complex Cloth: A Comprehensive Guide to Surface Design · Jane Dunnewold
Erika Carter: Personal Imagery in Art Quilts · Erika Carter
Inspiration Odyssey: A Journey of Self-Expression in Quilts · Diana Swim Wessel
The Nature of Design · Joan Colvin
Thread Magic: The Enchanted World of Ellen Anne Eddy · Ellen Anne Eddy
Velda Newman: A Painter's Approach to Quilt Design · Velda Newman with Christine Barnes

Appliqué in Bloom · Gabrielle Swain
Bargello Quilts · Marge Edie
Blockbender Quilts · Margaret J. Miller
Color: The Quilter's Guide · Christine Barnes
Colourwash Quilts · Deirdre Amsden
Freedom in Design · Mia Rozmyn
Hand-Dyed Fabric Made Easy · Adriene Buffington
Machine Needlelace and Other Embellishment Techniques · Judy Simmons
Quilted Sea Tapestries · Ginny Eckley
Watercolor Impressions · Pat Magaret & Donna Slusser
Watercolor Quilts · Pat Magaret & Donna Slusser

Many titles are available at your local quilt shop or where fine books are sold. For more information, write for a free color catalog to Martingale & Company, PO Box 118, Bothell, WA 98041-0118 USA.

U.S. and Canada, call 1-800-426-3126 for the name and location of the quilt shop nearest you.
Int'l: 1-425-483-3313
Fax: 1-425-486-7596
E-mail: info@martingale-pub.com
Web: www.patchwork.com